Christmas Spirits

Christmas Spirits

* * * * *

D. J. St. Amant

CREATIVE ARTS BOOK COMPANY
Berkeley • California 1999

Christmas Spirits is published by Donald S. Ellis
and distributed by Creative Arts Book Company

For Information contact:
Creative Arts Book Company
833 Bancroft Way
Berkeley, California 94710
(800) 848-7789

ISBN 0-88739-193-1
Library of Congress Catalog Number 98-74228

Printed in the United States of America

To

Kimberly Dolson

Marie Bonhomme

Cheryl Wiebe

Patricia Easton

I wish to thank the many people and friends who have patiently read drafts of these stories and offered feedback over the years. I also wish to thank my publisher and editors, especially Courtney Chittock, who was not only meticulously careful with every detail, but who pushed me to make my stories more of what I wanted them to be.

Contents

Christmas Spirits

Introduction:

Making Your Christmas a Sacred Celebration

For most of us, Christmas is a time of year to celebrate. It is a time filled with joy, warmth, excitement, memories of childhood, thoughts of those we love and those less fortunate, and a time of general goodwill.

I have always loved Christmas, since my earliest recollection, and from a young age, I wanted to host my own Christmas celebration without having my parents, siblings, or others I loved shape and determine what I should be doing and how. I wanted to do things my own way, making my own decisions based on the things that mattered to me. I did and do borrow from a lot of people I admire. But at Christmastime, I often felt like a child with adult visions of Christmas, yet confined to a child's environs, unable to make real these thoughts I had. I promised myself that one day I would create the Christmas I desired. Where this desire came from when I was so very young, I'm not sure. I can only say that in our house, all my siblings looked for ways to make Christmas something special for ourselves and our parents. So from a young age, a few of us would get up after my parents were asleep and add to the decorations or bring out extra gifts. One year we filled the living room with balloons; another, with streamers hung from the ceiling; another, with evergreens.

For me, Christmastime became an opportunity to make explicit the feelings I had toward those I liked, thanked, admired, and loved. In the beginning, with very little money for Christmas gifts, I wrote notes to those close to me to express what I felt. The closer someone was, the more I put into the note. As I got older and had more friends, the notes consumed more of my time. Eventually, I was having to take a lot of time away from my other writing in order to write (make) these notes (gifts).

I started to write more general notes, sometimes prose, sometimes poetry, sometimes essays. These were general enough that I could make the one gift suitable for most of my close friends. Over the years, my friends have enjoyed the gifts and I have really enjoyed writing them. I put my heart and soul into it. Very early on, reading them aloud on Christmas Eve became one of our traditions.

Even when I was no longer a penny-pinching writer, I continued writing these notes as part of our Christmas tradition. At some point, I turned my attention to short stories, and it was then I wrote a story with a Christmas setting and theme. It was a hit. So a Christmas story became part of our Christmas Eve tradition and still is to this day.

In our home, Christmas is the time of year when we give expression to the joys of life and the joys of being with those we love. We have an early Christmas dinner on Christmas Eve and follow it with singing carols, inside or outside, though the fresh air is usually welcomed. When we return, we read a Christmas story around the fireplace, then we open gifts and read cards. Also, we read selected poetry over dinner, or short pieces of prose, or humorous stories, and everyone is invited to make a toast or express a thought important to them. As well, we tell of past Christmases, special moments, and memories. We take time to salute those we love who were unable to attend and remember those we love who are no longer with us.

We change many things from year to year, including aspects of the gift-giving, dinner, and caroling. When friends are far away, we find ways of working them into our evening: a note or card read at the right moment, a toast, a photograph, a shared phone call, a special candle lit in their honor, a special piece of art displayed. We even toast lost friendships . . . those we loved or love who by choice (ours, theirs, or mutual) are no longer close to us.

As well, we decorate and prepare as best we can or as time permits. I'm always amazed by how much we do. But we love life, and life is full of values; to choose one particular value often results in not having time for another, so we don't want to drive ourselves crazy and show up on Christmas Eve or Christmas Day totally exhausted and unable to enjoy anything. And we don't wish to spend the weeks following Christmas recovering. In other words, we do not get too hung up on the exact details to follow, and we do invite changes from year to year. We try new things and add different ideas, knowing that the essence of the evening for us is intimate time shared together. With people we love sitting around the dining room table or mingling in the living room or library, everything else just doesn't matter a damn. We know it's going to be a wonderful evening, a celebration that seems to achieve the impossible by somehow surpassing the joys we've experienced in the past—whether or not the lamb was overcooked, the wine spilt, or we didn't sing for as long as we normally do . . . or we were short of time for buying gifts . . . or short of time for writing notes and cards . . . or that every year our conspiratorial felines fell our Christmas tree as we are about to dine . . .

We do not have a stressed-out Christmas despite all the things we do. The focus is on what matters to us: being together with those we love, and intimately celebrating the life we share and love. Running around with a pocketful of worries and last-minute concerns seems so petty and insignificant because frankly, that is not what life or Christmas is about.

Although our Christmas Eve Celebration is quite an evening to host in some respects, it is also quite easy. We live our daily lives a certain way, and at Christmastime, we heighten aspects of those ways where appropriate. By making explicit our thoughts in a toast, we give our thoughts a voice. By decorating the table in an unusual or festive manner, even in the simplest way, we express our respect for this celebration. By lighting the room with candles, listening to the children read a poem, having Christmas lights and a decorated tree, playing a special piece of music, dressing up formally for dinner, singing, dancing, and reading something close to the heart, we give voice to much of what we think and feel. The celebration need not be extravagant, it need only be sincere.

Here is where this collection of short stories and poems may help. It may bring to your Christmas celebration a sense of spirituality. Sitting together and listening to music, or to a story or poem read aloud, will definitely add intimacy to any evening. You will find these stories have a seriousness to them for the most part, an intensity I can neither rid myself of nor my writing. But I believe there is in these stories a sense that life is sacred. On the whole, they are easy reads: short, but not always sweet. Most can be read in less than half an hour, some much less. Reading aloud is a skill to cherish of course, and I can only promise you that most people get better at it the more they do it. These stories, although written primarily for adults, are quite easy for children to follow, and some stories feature children. I have found most children extremely receptive to all but one, "Christmas in So-Cal." As far as the poetry goes, many are quite short and focus on the lighter side of life, and they are open to all ages.

Through the years, my family and I have found that Christmas stories and poetry help create the sacredness we desire in our celebrations. The stories in this volume are not intended as "feel good" stories, although some will have that result. They are intended as stories to be experienced in themselves. You will have to decide for yourself how successful they are in that regard. But perhaps by reading aloud one of these stories, or selecting a few poems to read aloud, this book will help make your Christmas more relaxed, less hectic, and if the time is right, more sacred.

It is my sincere hope that in your home, Christmas is a celebration of the sacred joy of being alive, in love, and amongst others. I wish you all a Merry, Merry Christmas.

D. J. St. Amant

A Christmas Angel

Terence was exhausted.

He had barely slept since Monday; it was now Thursday morning, the day of Christmas Eve. He sat as if poised to act, yet he was too tired to move. This was the first time he had stopped to rest. He was sitting alone at a small table having a double espresso at Cafe du Monde. He leaned forward over the table, his stomach cramped in pain, his body ached. He had looked everywhere and done everything he could think of. He had been in tears since Monday evening. Now, he had no tears left, no feelings save one: anger. He was angry at the world and everyone in it. He was exhausted and needed sleep but knew he would hate himself for sleeping. He hoped the coffee would keep him awake so that he could consider what to do next. This was his third espresso; it wasn't working.

"I could strangle someone—" He stopped and shook his head at his own violent thoughts.

His voice mingled with the sound of someone playing Christmas carols on a piano, but he didn't hear. Everything seemed to swirl around him like floating sensations.

The last four weeks had been busier for him than at any other point in his career. He had worked on a business proposal for almost four months. He was a principal in a consulting firm and was one step from partnership. He was working on a huge add-on proposal and had put some ideas together with a

1

process improvement package for all levels of a national organization. He could not count the telephone calls, meetings, late nights, the hours spent on site with his partners and clients, everyone relying on him. It became his project. His knowledge, education, training, wit, patience, and experience were stretched to their limits. How many headaches did he have from this project alone? How many arguments with his partners in charge who thought this project should go otherwise? How many times had he taken it home with him only to snap at his wife about anything? Only to be impatient with his daughter? All because if this went well, he would be a partner by spring.

This week was the crucial time when he was to bring his client's board of directors in on the entire vision and all the process changes. He had everyone lined up for meetings and presentations at ten o'clock Tuesday morning, December twenty-second. If all went well, they could celebrate over the Christmas holidays.

Monday evening his seven-year-old daughter disappeared.

He simply had no pattern of anything in his life that could have prepared him for this. She was gone. In his tired state he could barely make himself comprehend. At first he simply denied it, as if she were just in the other room. But as time passed and she did not come out of her room, it sunk into his understanding. At that point he bolted into action, knocking on door after door, checking the neighborhood, the corner stores, and making calls to get others to help. The police came to get pictures and a description of what she was last wearing. He and his wife looked everywhere; everyone they knew helped them. They would have done anything to see her again . . .

Their child had renewed them, their love for each other and their love of life. She was adopted by them when she was twelve weeks old. She was healthy, happy—an endearing baby. They wanted her to be proud of her Korean heritage, so they named her Mei. She seemed heaven-sent. But despite all the care they took, Monday evening, after working himself to the point of exhaustion, he returned home so that he could get plenty of sleep before the morning presentations, and she was gone.

"Hello, hello," he said tiredly as he entered the apartment. Susan came from the kitchen and kissed him. Normally Mei would have come running to greet him too. Often she met him at the elevator.

"Where's Mei?"

"She was here listening to Christmas carols. Maybe she's asleep."

She wasn't.

They looked everywhere.

The apartment door had been unlocked. That was not unusual when he was getting home, but her white boots and winter coat were gone; they just didn't know what to think. She had been out of sight for less than twenty minutes, they calculated. She was sitting in the den listening to Christmas carols when he called to say he was leaving the office. Susan had been making dinner.

Now it was the day of Christmas Eve, and he was fully realizing how Mei had become his reason for celebrating Christmas, the reason for so much of what he did. Something dreadful must have happened to her, he thought. He felt sure someone had seen her, maybe could have done something about it. He had knocked on door after door throughout the entire apartment complex. One woman thought she saw her in the elevator; someone else saw a young child in the parking garage. No one else saw anything.

Terence and Susan looked everywhere they could think of and spoke to everyone they could. They checked the garages, walked the streets, and left pictures of her at stores, on streetlight poles, in apartment complexes and office buildings. They checked hallways, construction areas, garbage bins, back alleys, and the parking garages of other buildings.

People probably sat back and let a young girl be abducted, his tired mind thought. No one raising a finger, a voice, or even giving a second thought to what was happening before their eyes.

In his exhausted state, he was disgusted with everyone, including himself.

He looked at the others around him.

How many times had he sat like them, thinking those stories in the papers were of no concern? How many times had he, like them, avoided taking even simple steps so he could remain uninvolved? At work with colleagues; on the street with strangers. And at a bar after work two weeks ago, when he and his colleagues had ignored a young woman threatened by a man who seemed to be her boyfriend. They had all patted each other on the back and turned the other way.

"Just sitting here minding our own business," one of them had whispered.

But now it was his business . . . his little girl.

He shook his head at himself and at the others around him. Someone could have taken that first step, said that one word, acted on something unacceptable that was in front of their noses . . . like a seven-year-old disappearing.

"Mei . . ." he mumbled.

He hated to think of what had probably happened to her. He hated to think of the reports in the newspapers about various children who had been abducted, abused, and found in various mangled states in some underpass, bush, or garbage bin.

He looked blankly at the people sitting at the tables around him with their shopping bags and Christmas gifts . . . They were sitting much as he once would have, unconcerned by what was around him.

"Damn it all!" he shouted and pounded his fist on the table.

No one seemed to notice his outburst.

He leaned back in his chair to rest for a moment.

*****

A homeless man marched and stumbled along, his cold, numb feet shuffling to keep him in balance as his body wobbled and shifted from one side of the alley to the other. When he stood still, his body struggled with the effort it took, and his head swayed in small circles. He stood at attention, swaying, his body tormented by the circular inertia that seemed trapped inside of him. He started to move again and staggered along the alley as if drunk.

It was a miserably cold December morning in Toronto. He hated this time of year, he reminded himself. It was the only time when others would dare speak to him, wish him a Merry Christmas. It was always a bad, lonely time. It was at this time of year he first entered the underground world in which he now lived.

He stooped forward a little as if the weight of his hat was not only bending his ears, but was also causing his head to bow with the pressure. He stared down at the pavement in front of him and ground his teeth together to toughen his spirits against the cold weather and the seasonal cheer. His tattered coat was filthy, and he tried to pull it more tightly around himself as he walked into the cold wind that channelled its way through the alley. He was in a hateful mood.

Although he looked old, he was a middle-aged man and not unhealthy. He could have been good-looking, except that thoughts have a face. He attempted to march as if he were a soldier, but his numb body and bitter spirit seemed unaware of such actions; he stumbled to where the alley ended. When he noticed a clean sidewalk beneath his bare feet, he tried to stand upright as if at attention. He stopped for a moment and forced his shoulders back as he fought to still his inner sway. He tried to raise his head.

He stepped off the sidewalk and staggered across the cold pavement of the street.

By street standards this man was rich; he had two residences. One was an abandoned car in the courtyard of a filthy alley, hidden behind a cluster of restaurants. The car was a convertible with a smashed window; this was his front door, for he could enter it without making any noise. The front seat was his guest room, the back seat his living room, and the trunk his bedroom. When he wanted to sleep there, he entered his front door, crawled into his living room, pulled the back seat forward, squeezed himself into his bedroom, and replaced the back seat so that no one could see him in there. His other residence was below the streets, in the storm sewers of Toronto. Last night he had slept in the car.

Normally, when he found himself in this alley, he would enter the parking garage of the Manulife Centre, where he had removed a manhole cover at the end of a hidden corridor; it was a shortcut entrance to his home beneath the city. Today, he felt the cold in a way he was not accustomed to. His feet were not concerned with his regular routes and desired to get out of the freezing cold; this left him walking straight up the stairs of the Manulife Centre. He pulled open the door and, without thinking about what he was doing, entered the warmth of the mall as quickly as he could. He felt the warmth of the entrance heaters immediately, which made him shiver and shake.

His mind seemed to rejoin his body, and he realized he did not belong here. He had not taken this route in a long time. He had wanted to go to his second home, the sewer, but his frozen, unconscious feet were seeking relief. For a moment he thought he would at least search the garbage cans in the cleaner confines of the mall because there was nothing more to eat in the alley. The owners of the restaurants had stopped putting out their refuse to stop rummagers from going through it. But upon seeing the clean floors and the shiny glass he reconsidered and stopped at the second set of doors. He was about to turn back, but there was a crowd of people coming in, and he could feel the cold from outside. He moved forward instead. An image that was not quite a thought entered his mind. The image was of him escaping these confines through the other side of the mall. As he walked into the mall, he saw pastries behind glass, and more pastries piled on the marble countertop at Cafe du Monde. He stopped for a moment to see, to smell; he closed his eyes and held his breath. A soft pain pricked his eyes beneath his closed eyelids. The aromas had a power he had not experienced in some time, and he became still, content to smell, for it evoked pleasant memories. He heard someone's fingers lightly touching a piano in the corner, and he opened his eyes and looked beyond the escalators to see a white-haired woman playing. As he listened, his nose told him there was a scent of fresh flowers in the air. He stood, content to smell and listen. He had smelled and heard only the streets for so long that the aromas and the music continued to flash images in his mind of when he was a younger man. He shook his head to ease his trance and turned toward the serving counter of Cafe du Monde. He remembered that one of the clerks had given him a French pastry once, but he could not accurately recall any details, even if the waiter did look familiar. This waiter giving him a French pastry was the only kindness anyone had shown him, he thought.

"Ever," he mumbled.

It was more a moan than a word.

He ground his teeth together in agitation, but the aroma of the espresso being made seemed to ease his desire to scream. He stood staring at the large copper and brass espresso machine. The aroma made him dizzy, and beyond it there was the smell of freshly steamed milk. It was an exquisite sweetness he could not recall tasting, but he watched as it was added to a cup of coffee on the counter, only a few steps away.

He growled, swung his arms as if punching the air, and moved away from the counter lest he think a cup of this were for him and become determined to take it. He turned toward the other mall exit but stopped. He grimaced as if in pain, clenched his teeth, and rubbed his face as he thought of how it hurt being here. Everything seemed so clean, so decorated, so colorful and from his past. He could feel his stomach churning as he looked at others as if daring them to come near him that he might scream at them or spit in their faces.

He clenched his fists.

There was desperation and fear in his anger; he feared everyone, especially himself. Self-loathing is a kind of violence waiting to act, a thought ready to slash out with vehemence. Self-loathing finds a ready target in random things and people, thus he stood there for a moment daring anyone to come near him or gaze in his direction that he might give his anger a voice in action.

He looked around, then stumbled forward toward the mall exit at the far end of the concourse. He was cold and hungry. On his way to the exit, he stopped at a garbage can between the escalators going up and down. He groaned as he looked at others who were there. He gnashed his teeth together with the thought that it was his own ongoing choices that made the sewers his home and forced him to search in these garbage cans. Because such thoughts have a face, this man was ugly. He growled as he lifted the top off the garbage can and stuck his head down inside.

* * * *

Terence had fallen asleep but was not sure for how long. He raised his head from the table and rubbed his eyes. His third espresso was sitting in front of him. In one quick gulp, he swallowed the cold coffee and pushed the cup away. He thought he should get up and return to the apartment, but he was too tired to move, and he didn't know if he had the strength to listen to Susan's self-deprecating rants. Maybe he would wait for her to meet him here.

He looked at the folded newspaper in front of him.

"Girl Still Missing," one headline stated.

He pushed the paper away.

He looked around at the mall, the cafe tables, and the escalators. The mall was busy, and at first he barely noticed something moving in darkness and filth. Then he saw that the darkness was a dirty coat and the filth was straggly hair and an unwashed face. For a moment he had to assure himself that this was a living human being.

Terence looked right at the homeless man as he walked toward the escalators. The man had a lifeless stare, a look of blind hatred toward everything around him. His harsh expression appeared to be carved into his leathery skin by the cold wind. It was difficult to distinguish the parts of his leathery skin darkened by the elements from where he had not washed. His scruffy, curly beard was unkempt, except where his hands wiped his chapped lips, and the moisture and friction bleached the hair around his mouth an auburn color. His mouth was like a dark cave whose incoming light was not reflected out. His nose gave his looks the faintest refined promise, for it was thin and delicate, yet his nostrils were black from living in the sewers. He wore a black bandanna that kept his straggly hair from covering his eyes completely, but it was difficult to see, for his skin was the same color. The whites of his eyes were red, and he had an eery way of staring that suggested his focus was more inward, but without missing anything going on around him.

Terence noticed, first in himself and then in others, a desire to look away and evade notice of this man. Yet everyone noticed him despite not wanting to. They moved away from him so that he walked alone, in the space around him. He stopped at the garbage can between the escalators and separated the flow of people going up and coming down. He looked around in anger, as if to flaunt what he felt; he had no shame. It was almost pride, Terence thought. Knowing what he was about to do would bother others, the man lifted the lid of the garbage can, raised his head for a moment, growled, then stuck his head inside to see if he could find anything. He pulled out half a muffin dripping with coffee, a piece of stale cheddar cheese, a slightly eaten apple, and a small styrofoam bowl of milk and soggy cereal. He put the muffin, cheese, and apple into his pocket, then took the plastic spoon and ravished the milk and cereal. While he ate, he stared around, daring anyone to come near or look at him. Everyone seemed to sense this man's threat and stayed away. But even with averted eyes, they couldn't avoid noticing that he had taken the styrofoam bowl out of the garbage and was eating the cereal with the long, yellow plastic spoon that had been left with it.

Terence shook his head and watched others as they made

their way through the busy mall. He noticed a large, friendly woman coming down the escalators, waving good-bye to someone on the floor above. As the escalator carried her down, she looked up at the round skylight above as it cast its pleasant, dispersed light across the concourse. She was still looking up at the skylight when the escalator delivered her onto the unmoving, marble-tiled floor. She stumbled to regain her balance, stepping firmly on the foot of a short, well-dressed gentleman. Crying out loudly at the pain caused by the weight that had landed on his foot, he blushed at his outburst.

"I'm dreadfully sorry," she said, raising her voice as he moved away from her.

Other people passing by skirted around her. Terence watched as she tried to approach the injured gentleman to see if he was okay. He continued walking away, now with a definite limp. Reluctantly, having failed to have her apology accepted, she proceeded the other way, looking back to show him her concern. When he disappeared around the corner, she turned abruptly, only to be confronted by the sight of the man from the streets eating a soggy bowl of cereal.

"Oh my God," she said aloud.

She looked at him, trying to hide her revulsion, yet she could not find within herself the strength to look away. She stared with pity and disbelief, then shook herself and fumbled with her purse to get her wallet so that she could give him some money.

The sounds that came from the mouth and throat of this man were the growls of the sewers and the underground. It was something awakened from these depths that reached up and slapped the lady's face, knocking her back. She fell onto the marble-tiled floor. He turned to kick her as she fell, but instead, his bare foot passed by her head and hit her purse; the contents scattered across the floor, and everyone turned toward the awakened beast.

The man stood still for a moment, like an animal awaiting attack.

Terence stood up.

The man looked around, dropped the styrofoam bowl of cereal, and ran.

Terence ran after him.

The man from the street heard the footsteps of someone chasing him and voices yelling. His fear grew.

Terence ran as fast as he could.

The street person moaned aloud and ran faster.

When an angry body is awakened in fear, muscles are taut and at full readiness without preparation. Fear has a veto power over all concerns of comfort and signals of pain. The man bolted like a wild animal. He was already down the stairs to the subway level.

"Stop him," he heard someone yell.

His heart pounded, and his mind formed one order: Run.

He repeated this order to himself over and over and listened for nothing else except the footsteps behind him. He pushed himself to run faster. He ran straight past the large flower boxes of purple chrysanthemums which lined the walls, and he bumped people who shouted as he fought to get by them. He heard those same sounds repeated behind him. He was a wild animal possessed by fear.

Running, he saw the stores as blurred colors and shapes. He noticed that beyond the bank machine in front of him the corridor continued left and right. He thought only of the underground, his home. No one would find him there. He turned right, bumping two people, who fell. Then he ran between a couple holding hands and knocked the coffee out of the hands of another person who stood beside them in front of the Timothy's Cafe counter. He turned into a crowd and bolted through the underground entrance to the Holt Refrew Centre.

He ran into the crowded, sunken underpass and took the wheelchair ramp. He pushed a man making his way down in a wheelchair and sent him rolling out of control through the other side. He faintly heard the curses of anger of those behind him and listened for the sounds of footsteps as he repeated his order to run to himself.

Lights, glass, mirrors, Christmas decorations, and the marble-tiled floor became one large blur. He ran between people, knocking them over, spinning them around, sending bags and gifts whirling into the air. He ran through free-standing signs of advertising that were in the middle of the corridor. Beams of light bounced off pieces of chrome and made everything in front of him seem small and confined. He felt caged. He swung his arms harder and groaned aloud at anyone in his path. People sensed him as if they felt a change in the air pressure. They moved, shifting with the force of his direction before they saw him, and thus, as the terrace became more crowded, he seemed to ease his way through more quickly. The footsteps behind him were becoming fainter.

"Stop him," Terence yelled and repeated.

But no one would dare; this man hated enough to bite his way through the crowd if he had to, Terence thought as he tried valiantly not to lose sight of him.

The man ran to his right, encountering another sunken underpass. The floor turned brown, the ceiling stucco-white, and the walls red brick with brass trim. He saw a flash of light that was an exit to the street, but it was blocked by the many people coming in. He kept running.

His fear of being apprehended made his anger a blind rage.

He ran between a mother and child, spinning them both and knocking their shopping bags out of their hands. He knocked over two young boys, who screeched out in pain. He saw a crowded escalator carrying people up, but he bypassed this congested corridor. The exit to the street on his left would mean a change of direction: His anger drew a line; he ran straight ahead.

Now more and more people seemed to obstruct him, though they sensed him coming and tried to turn away. His pace was starting to slow; he was sure the footsteps behind him were drawing nearer.

He ran for the subway entrance. He barged through a door,

knocking a young girl over, then stumbled down the stairs. He ran to the exit turnstile, and without losing a step, he put his hands up on either side and hopped over. He turned to his left, to the escalator, and ran a couple of steps down before he realized that the escalator and the people on it were all coming up. He ran harder and shoved people aside using sheer force. At the bottom of the escalator he swung left onto the Yonge southbound platform. He sprinted to the edge of the crowded platform and started running along the yellow warning track. Nervously, everyone backed away from the edge; the train could be heard approaching the station.

"Look out!" people screamed.

"Stop him," yelled Terence, following behind.

The train was approaching, slowing down as it reached the station. The man ran to the far end of the platform to a small metal gate that said: Danger. Do Not Enter. He turned and looked back at the crowded platform. The people seemed to sense he was looking at them. They stared at him in a moment of silence, in a moment of pity, in a moment of fear and disbelief as he stood in front of the restraining gate. He looked at the crowd as if addressing each and every one of them. He clenched both fists at his sides and uttered a deep sound that was more animal than human, more sewer than animal. It reverberated throughout the halls of the subway station.

"Faaarrrrgh!"

Terence approached the edge of the platform and ran toward him.

The man turned, hopped the gate, leapt off the platform, and ran along the tracks to where the tunnel swerved inward. He was gone.

"That way," said Terence as several policemen approached him and followed the man.

"We'll take it from here, sir," one of them said to Terence.

Alarms had been sounded, and the train pulled into the station very slowly. Terence stood there trying to catch his breath. He hadn't run like that in years and felt faint. Panting, he watched the policemen who were following along the train tracks. One of them slowly stepped over to the other side of the tracks and shone his flashlight. He called to the others to follow into the darkness of the underground subway.

No one had lifted a finger to help, Terence thought to himself as he turned back.

"Mei," he said and started to cry. He buried his face in his hands for a moment and then slowly started walking back through the subway station. He stopped and held the wall as everything around him seemed to spin. He leaned over; he was sweating profusely. When he caught his breath, he made his way up the stairs and out into the cold air.

The cold felt good after his exertion, but he was not dressed to be out. The biting wind seemed to pass right through him, and he started to shiver. As his breathing returned to normal, he hurried along Bloor Avenue and entered the Manulife Centre. Inside, making his way toward the residential elevators, he walked by the woman who had been hit by the street person. She was talking to a police officer and someone from mall security.

"I'm fine, really," he heard her say. "What he did was wrong, but I don't need to add to his woes. Trust me, I'm fine. Let's leave it at that."

Terence was standing by the elevators, waiting to go up, when Susan came out of an elevator going down.

They looked at each other, held out their arms, and sobbed. When the tears seemed controllable, he took her by the hand and led her to Cafe du Monde. She sat at the table where he had been earlier, and he went to the counter and ordered an espresso and a cappuccino. As they sat sipping their coffee, he told her about the homeless man he had chased.

"Maybe it was a crazy idea to chase him, but he hit a woman and knocked others over. And everyone stood there. Didn't bat an eye or lift a finger. No one, can you believe that? No wonder a seven-year-old girl can just vanish. How do we sleep with ourselves at night? Everyone saw this guy, everyone.

He flagrantly bumps into people, hits a woman, knocks her over, and everyone just turns the other way to ignore it. No wonder people are able to get away with whatever the hell they want. There is something very wrong here," he said bitterly.

He looked at her.

She was mumbling to herself.

He became quiet.

"What have we done, Mei?" she asked. "How could we have failed you? How do you lose your only child? Why did I ever stop going to the elevator with you? A few moments more in the kitchen? What was so important in the kitchen? What madness is this?"

He didn't know what to say or do. He bit his lip to hold back the tears.

"How often did I encourage her to dress up for her father coming home from work?" she continued. "To greet him at the door? The elevator? Why did I let her start going into the halls alone?"

He lowered his head.

Her mumbling grew weaker, and she waved her hands over her cappuccino as if directing it to do something.

She became quiet and still.

They sat in silence.

She reached for her cup.

"I would do anything just to have another chance," she said.

He reached over the table and put his arms on her shoulders. "We just have to hope," he said.

"Hope . . ." she said blankly.

She buried her face in her hands.

* * * * *

Running along the middle of the tracks in his bare feet, the man reached the point where the platforms were now out of sight. He looked back to see if anyone could see him and then crossed over onto the other tracks and stepped into a small cove that was built into the side of the northbound tunnel. There he turned his attention to two old adjoining doors that did not quite meet. The space between those doors revealed a corridor on the other side. He put his hands into the space between the doors, and with all his strength, he pulled one door open wide enough for him to slip through.

On the other side of the door there was light. His rage was subsiding. He stopped there for a moment to regain his breath.

"He must have crossed over," he heard someone say. "Can we get in there?"

He ran along the lit corridor to a large metal door. It was locked. Out of his tattered pants he pulled two thin pieces of metal. He unlocked the door in moments. Beyond the door there was a long staircase that ended at yet another door. Beyond that door was the entrance to his home. He ran down the stairs.

"In there," he heard voices echo behind him.

Again he quickly unlocked the door, and once on the other side, he lifted the heavy manhole cover. He quickly slipped down into the storm sewers in the heart of Toronto. As he descended the stairs, he opened and closed his eyes to adjust to the darkness. He could hear someone walking over the manhole cover above him, blocking the few rays of light that were streaming in.

"Hurry up . . ." he heard a deep voice say.

He quickly descended the next few stairs, lowered his head, and started to run again.

He knew the sewers as one knows one's own neighborhood. He ran through these rounded halls of filth as if it were natural to his body. Like a rodent, he had adjusted to the sewers in many ways. He could see quickly, got his bearings, and headed toward the spot he called home. There he had set up a hammock in a deep, dark corner just beyond a manhole cover. From high above, this manhole cover acted as a skylight, always emitting four lines of light—white sunlight during the day, yellow streetlights at night. From his hammock, everything approaching this spot was visible, while he remained unseen. And in a few emergencies, the manhole cover had served him well as an exit. He was running through his neighborhood toward his home. He heard voices. The others had entered, but they were hesitant.

"Forget it. We'll never find him," he thought he heard one of them say.

He looked back, and in the light of the opening, he could see someone down at the bottom of the stairs leaning in but holding firmly onto a rung of the stairs. He turned and ran. They were right, he thought, they would never find him.

He continued running until he turned several corners and entered what he called the Black Hole. The Black Hole storm sewer was a long, elevated excess drainage sewer that had no lights and no manhole covers. Two people could pass each other without knowing the other was there. He slowed down, and at a dark hole in the wall, stepped up into it. He walked in utter blackness until he could finally see shades of minimal light at the far end. He moved to the right, crossed the drain pipe, walked along the upward slanted storm sewer for a short distance, and emerged into a large main drain sewer. His home was just beyond the next corner.

The four beams of light formed round circles that raced down into the depths of his front porch. In the absolute darkness of the space behind it, this light created ambient lighting for hundreds of feet in each direction. Light in the sewers was not well nourished, but beneath this manhole cover the light looked soft and warm. This spot was the entrance porch to his home. He walked, turned the corner, and stopped suddenly. He heard a noise ahead of him and the echo of it behind him; something did not look right beneath the beams of light. He stood perfectly still.

* * * * *

Mei felt like crying; it was the softest thing she had ever felt.

She sat on the bed beside her school friend, Michelle Burton. She was staying with Michelle this Saturday morning while her mother had her hair done. Michelle lived in the same apartment building. She had asked for a kitten for Christmas and today had brought the kitten home from the store. The kitten's back and crown were grey. Its face, underside, and legs were white except for small oval spots of grey that covered the back side of each paw and its nose.

The small kitten squeaked a meow at Mei. It rubbed its head against her hand and leg. Then it crawled up her pants as if it were climbing some large tree, stopping for breath and in fear of falling, digging in its claws as hard as it could. Once it reached her lap, it climbed her sweater and pawed at her lips. It meowed as if it were complaining, as if there were something wrong and somehow Mei could make it better. Mei gently returned the kitten to her lap. It kneaded her leg before getting comfortable, then looked up at her with its sad, grey-green eyes.

Mei could not speak. She felt an outpouring of emotion. She just wanted to cry. This was the most beautiful thing she had ever seen. Michelle put one arm around her shoulder and with the other gently stroked the back of the kitten while it purred.

"She likes you," said Michelle.

Mei and Michelle had been friends since the first grade. Mei took to kissing everyone she met when she first went to school. The boys had run away, the girls had giggled. Michelle had cried. She became Mei's best friend.

"What are you going to call her?" asked Mei.

"I don't know yet. I want to call her Samantha, but Daddy says it's too long a name."

"Samantha's a nice name," said Mei.

"Yeah, I like it," said Michelle.

Mei sat with Michelle and was quiet. For the first time, a serious, dark cloud appeared overhead. The world had been a glorious and happy place, but now she would never be happy again, she thought.

"I want a kitten too," she said to Michelle and started to cry.

"It's okay," said Michelle. "Just ask your mom."

Mei could only shake her head. Her mother had already warned her she could not have a kitten.

When Mei's mother picked her up before lunch time, Mei immediately asked again.

"Michelle has one."

"We are not going to," said her mother.

"But I want a kitten," said Mei.

"Well, you may want one, but we are not getting one."

"Why not?"

"We've explained to you that there are no pets allowed in this apartment building."

"But everyone has one," she complained, "and so does Michelle Burton."

"But they are not supposed to," said her mother.

"But why do they if they're not supposed to? Are they bad?"

"No . . ." her mother said. "If Michelle's mother doesn't mind Michelle having one, that is her own business, but that does not mean you can then have one too. I'm afraid you will have to wait till you are older to understand, my little girlie."

"I hate having to wait. When I'm older, I'm going to have a kitty, you just wait and see."

That silenced her mother.

"I want a kitty," she chanted over and over, throughout the afternoon.

Then before dinner, her mother scolded her.

"I do not want to hear another word about wanting a kitten. Do you understand me, young lady? That is the end of it."

"But I want one," Mei cried.

"That's it," said her mother. She took Mei's hand and led her to her room. "You may come out of your room when you are prepared to behave properly."

This had never happened before. It was all her heart could bear; she cried and cried with her face down on her pillow. It was as if the whole world had darkened.

Her mother very gently closed the door.

In the evening, when Mei finally came out of her room, she was all the more determined to have a kitten; she would just not tell her mother. One day, she would go and buy one at the store with her own money and bring it home to keep in her room.

That night, she dreamt she had done just that.

The next day, on Sunday, when her father returned from the office in the middle of the afternoon after having to work most of the weekend, he gave her a stuffed kitten that was white and had blue-buttoned eyes.

"I want a real kitten," she said, then broke into tears. "I want a kitty. I want a kitty . . ."

"For Christ's sake, Terry," said her mother. Then her mother sternly took the stuffed animal and roughly handed it back to her father and again lead her to her room. She was told she could come out when she was prepared to forget about a kitten.

"Never," she whispered resolutely to herself. She did not come back out that evening. She fell asleep on her bed after crying for quite some time, and when she awoke in the early morning, she had her pyjamas on.

Before eating breakfast, her mother told her to get dressed up because they were going out to do some Christmas shopping. She liked shopping and put on a dress she liked. After breakfast they went down the elevator and made their way outside; it was snowing. Mei raised her hands into the air and looked up. She opened her mouth wide in hopes of catching some of these large white snowflakes. Some snowflakes landed on her face, eyes, and ears first. Then finally she felt the tickling cold of them on her tongue. She giggled and cheered.

"Come on," coaxed her mother, "we have Christmas shopping to do."

Mei walked toward her mother on the sidewalk, but then she thought she heard something.

"Wait," she shouted.

She thought she heard the meow of a kitten.

"Mommy, listen," she said.

They listened together to the faint meow. They looked in the shrubs; they looked around some pine trees. Mei looked down through the grid of the exhaust vent of the underground parking garage, and just off the side at the bottom, there was a small white kitten.

"Mommy," she screamed.

Her mother looked down too.

"How on earth did a kitten get in there?" she asked, annoyed.

She assured Mei that she would speak to the parking lot attendant to get it out of there.

"But we're not keeping it," she warned, then looked down at Mei. "Look, we'll make sure they get the kitten out of there, then we'll start our shopping, okay?"

Mei nodded sadly.

They reentered their building and went down into the parking garage, and her mother told the man in the booth about the trapped kitten in the exhaust vent. At first he seemed to think they wanted directions.

"Yes, well, go through that door behind the private parking, right there, in that corner . . . I don't think it's locked." He pointed to an open door and smiled at Mei.

"No, no, listen. We don't want to get the kitten out ourselves," her mother said. "We were hoping you could get someone to get it out of there."

"Oh," he said. "Well, I suppose we could, for you ladies," he said, smiling. "What apartment are you in? I'll have one of the fellas fetch it and take it up to you."

He put out his hand and leaned through the window on the other side of his booth to accept someone's parking ticket and payment, then pushed the button to lift the parking gate. When he finished, he turned to face them.

"It's not ours," said her mother. "We just thought the kitten would freeze to death if left in there."

"Not yours?" he asked.

"No, it isn't," her mother said.

"And you don't want it?" he asked.

"No," her mother said and then added, "we can't."

"What exactly would I be doing with the little creature then?" he asked her.

"Surely someone will want it," her mother offered. "My daughter was worried about what would happen to the poor thing."

"Why don't you let her take the kitty home? Bet you'd like to have a kitty—" he said to Mei.

"Yes," she quickly answered.

"That's not the point," her mother said. "We're just worried about the kitten. We were walking by, and my daughter spotted it, trapped in there, and we were hoping one of you could get it out of there, that's all. Perhaps we should call the Humane Society."

"Oh . . ." he said and turned his head back toward the next car that had pulled up to the window.

Her mother took her hand. "They'll get the kitten out of there," she said.

They took a different way home, so Mei didn't get a chance to check on the kitten. But she had a plan. Her dad was going to be getting home from work that evening, so she would look to see if the kitten was still there before meeting her dad at the elevator. She knew she couldn't let her mother know about it, though. She took the milk left in her glass and poured it into a small plastic sandwich bag and secured it with a twist tie. She put on a dress and shoes as she usually did when her father was arriving home. She sat on the sofa in the den and listened to the Christmas carols being played on the radio.

Then she heard the telephone ring.

"He'll be here soon," her mother said from the kitchen once she was off the phone.

Her dad always phoned to let them know he was leaving the office and would be home in fifteen minutes.

"Okay," said Mei over the music.

She quietly went to the front closet and put on her white winter boots and gloves and her black coat. Then she quietly unlocked the apartment door, opened it, and slipped out. Nervously, she walked to the elevator, pressed the button, and, when a car stopped for her moments later, got in. She stepped between the two adults talking inside, pressed the button for the ground floor, and turned to look up at the lights like the adults did. She got out at the ground level in the front lobby of her apartment building, turned right, and entered the Concourse level of shops in the Manulife Centre. She made her way to the exit doors and stepped outside.

In the darkness and cold, she went to the side of the building and over to the steel grid of the exhaust vent from underground. She knelt down on the grid and peered in for a moment; she could not see anything. Then, when she was about to go back inside, she heard the faintest meow she had ever heard. She started to cry.

"It's okay," she assured the kitten, "it's okay."

She stood up and ran straight for the exit ramp of the underground parking lot.

The ramp had an elevated curb, a narrow strip of concrete that prevented cars from hitting the wall. She ran on this strip of concrete, and a car honked as she ran by. At the first level of parking she ran to the stairwell. She went down to the second level, where the large exhaust fan was, and went over to the fan, but it was covered with thick metal bars. She looked inside to see the kitten; it was lying on its side in a corner. She turned back and went to a door in the corner and tried it; it was locked. She went back to the stairs and down a corridor and tried each door. The doors were locked. She turned back and tried another corridor, and along it one door had a mop handle stuck into it to keep it open. She opened the door and entered a dark corridor that smelled strange. She followed it to the end of a corridor that had a staircase going up along the exhaust vent and a door beneath it. She turned the door handle, pushed the door open, and entered.

When she entered, the white kitten did not move. The noise from the turning fan was loud. Only when she got close did the kitten hear her. It seemed to gather its strength and started to meow in short bursts, as if she had done it an injustice by leaving it down here for so long. Slowly, as she petted it, its meows grew softer and more forgiving. She pressed the kitten against her chest and kissed its head. Then she sat down on the dirty, dust-covered floor and took out her plastic sandwich bag of milk. As she opened it, the kitten weakly stuck its face into the milk and lapped it up. It began to purr. She let the kitten lap up the milk for a few minutes and then twist-tied the bag closed again and put it back into her coat.

"Let's go," she said.

She wasn't sure what she would tell her mother yet, but she knew she would be in a lot of trouble. She was hoping to get the kitten into her room without her mother noticing, but she wasn't sure she would succeed. Because she had never disobeyed her mother, she wasn't sure what this meant; that made her worry. She walked toward the door, and the fan stopped. She could hear voices. She panicked. In fear she turned and ran past the large exhaust vent to a short tunnel and a small, half-sized grey door. She turned the door handle. It was locked. She heard someone approaching, and in fear she pulled the door toward her; to her surprise it opened. She stepped through and closed the door behind her; it clicked shut. She waited for her eyes to adjust. Then she walked along a short passageway and followed the stairs down. As she walked down in the darkness, the air grew cool and had a terrible smell. She held her nose, tucked her kitten into her jacket, and descended the rest of the stairs to a spot where one dim yellow light lit the area around a large, circular hole in the floor. Down one side of the uncovered hole there was a ladder made of metal bars. The distance between each rung was large. Like the distance between the metal bars on telephone poles, she thought. She turned around and went back up the stairs to the door. It was locked. She tried to push it open, but it remained closed. She knocked on it hard with her fists, but no one came. She started to cry. She stood there banging on the door, yelling for help.

After what seemed like a long time, she walked back down the stairs. At the hole with the metal bars for a staircase, she looked in to see if she could see anything. She couldn't. The stairs led to a passageway that disappeared into the darkness. As she stood there, her kitten crawled out of her coat and onto the top of her shoulder. She screeched and tried to grab it. It slipped off her shoulder and slid into the darkness of the hole.

Mei screamed, then lightly started slapping herself on the head over, and over as if to wake herself.

At many points in her life, she had realized that tears and wishes did not change certain things, especially if her mother and father were not around. Right now she wanted to cry. She held back her tears with the strength of two words: "Not now!" And sometimes with a third: "Soon!" She suppressed her fear as best she could and started humming Christmas carols incoherently as she descended one rung of the stairs at a time. The distance between each rung was large, and it took her a long time to reach the next one. She continued humming with a growing determination to master her fear, and she kept looking up to the dull light above.

She puckered her lips and kissed them together in a squeaking noise to attract her kitten. "You're going to be okay," she said. "I'll give you some more milk."

She reached one stair where she could not feel the next one. She stretched her foot down, but there seemed to be no more rungs. She stared down below, hoping she could see something. She could still see light faintly above her, but she could not see anything below. Mei called to the kitten and thought she heard its weak meow. She held onto the metal rung, stretched her legs down as far as she could, and dropped a short distance to the floor below.

She rubbed her hurt elbow and quickly looked each way. She puckered her lips and kissed them together again and again.

The kitten rubbed the side of its face against her leg.

"I almost lost you," she cried as she picked it up and stood there in the dark.

Her eyes seemed to adjust, and after a time, she could make out the two walls. She started walking, believing that if she walked, she would find her way out farther ahead.

After a while, she grew tired and cold. She just kept walking and walking, lost and scared. She entered areas where there was no light and no sound except the echo of dripping water and her steps. Occasionally there were groans, as if the earth below her had sent out warnings of danger or cries for help. At some places she stopped to rest. In utter darkness at one of her stopping points, she had to fight off a cat to save her kitten, as a mother would have fended for her own child. If she had been told that the cat she fought off was a sewer rat, she would not have persevered.

She didn't know how long she had been down in this place nor how far she had walked. She was hungry, dizzy, and very weak, and so was her kitten. At some point, she came across a spot where she could see bright beams of light, like streams of water, pouring down from far, far above. The light seemed warm, and her kitten meowed as if it sensed her hope. She was so weak . . . and in her weakened state, she thought to try and breast-feed her kitten as her mother had told her all mothers do, but it was all she could do to hold her kitten. She sat in the beams of light to rest, hoping . . . She tried to keep herself awake and incoherently sang songs to ease her fears. She was afraid the large cat that made funny noises would return and come after her kitten. She imagined herself with a sword to fight it off, but the sword became a pillow . . . and then she fell asleep trying to swing the pillow that was too heavy for her at the large cat with red eyes, sharp teeth, and an awful voice.

* * * * *

Standing perfectly still in the darkness of the storm sewer, he clenched his hands into fists and held his breath. He was not sure how anyone had found him or this spot so close to his underground home. He waited to hear other sounds, wondering whether to go forward or back. He waited, hoping to see better, or hoping this vision would just vanish. From where he stood, the four beams of light made clear the outline of an angel.

She was looking up toward the light, as if she were about to be lifted. Her little face seemed to control the light, as if it followed her head movements. Yet she frowned with concern, as though disappointed by being unable to float up toward the light. The white ruffled fringe on her black winter coat shone, as did her white gloves. She was sitting slouched against the wall, looking up while holding something carefully to her breast. Her black hair, pulled away from her face, was braided in the middle and tied with a ribbon. When she squinted to look up, her eyes became lighted circles and her nose a silver button. She moved her head; the light seemed to play with the fringe of her coat, the ribbon in her hair, and her white-gloved hands, which held a white ball of moving fur. The light danced on her shoulders and seemed to sing to her as she sat and listened . . .

From the darkness, he watched this angel slouched against the wall of the entrance to his home. He was sure she would be lifted up at any moment and carried away, but she did not move. He did not know what to do. He looked down at his tattered clothes and his ravaged appearance. He swallowed and took a deep breath. He wiped his lips and tried to straighten his matted hair by patting it. He brushed his beard back with his fingers and licked his hands in an attempt to keep it there. He tried to run his fingers through his hair to untangle the mess, but it was impossible. He tried to brush the filth from the cuffs of his shirt and coat, as well as the dirt on his trousers. He rubbed his fingers across his teeth to clean them, then straightened out his bushy eyebrows by pressing them down.

He took his first steps toward her.

She turned to face him, hearing his approach.

"I'm lost," she mumbled in exhaustion.

He felt moisture in the corners of his eyes.

He buried his face in his hands in an attempt to calm himself. Again he desperately tried to run his fingers through his wretched hair. He could not.

This angel speaks to me, he thought. Her words sounded like a song, a song answering a prayer in his thoughts. This angel was singing to him. Yet her song seemed sad, as if something were wrong.

"I want my mommy," she moaned.

He did not know what to do.

She sang tones that sounded like words. Never had he heard sounds so beautiful, notes so full, rich, melodious, and meaningful to his heart. He thought he should offer his hand, but even in this minimal light his hands looked dirty, his fingernails unclean; he thought to cut them off.

"Where's my mommy?"

More songs, he thought, but he did not speak. He hesitated. He tried to clear his throat so that he might say something to this angel, but he had no words and did not wish to growl. He extended his hand for her to take; he dropped to one knee before her and lowered his head. She stayed slouched against the wall as if stuck there.

"I want my mommy," she cried.

When she tried to get up on her feet, she stumbled. He quickly put out his arms and held her. He took out of his pocket the half piece of coffee-soaked muffin and gave it to her. She gobbled a piece of it down and offered some to her kitten. The kitten smelled it but did not respond. He took out a small piece of cheese and crushed it in the palm of his hand and placed it before the nose of the kitten. The kitten, without sense, bit at everything as if in a daze. It fed on the cheese and meowed in its scolding tone until its squawks were replaced with a faint, rolling purr. When the kitten had finished the cheese and the child the muffin, he took out the half-eaten apple and handed it to her, hoping she would not see how brown it was. She immediately ate it, core, stem, and all. When she finished, she returned the kitten to her coat. He wanted this angel to follow him, but she was weak on her feet and held his arm for balance. He felt her icy cold hands through her white gloves and held her hands for a moment to warm them. He stood up, took off his jacket, and wrapped it around her. It covered her completely and dragged past her feet. She shivered.

"I want my mommy," she groaned.

He looked down at her and was still unable to speak. He lifted her up into his arms. He was not sure what to do. He waited and stood there looking at the angel in his arms. Then he looked in the direction from which he had come. He held her gently against his chest, listening to the sounds she sang, but he was not able to understand. And as she continued these sounds with each breath, he started to walk. After the first few steps, he walked faster, until he built his walk into a run.

In exhaustion, the child nestled against his chest, holding tightly onto her kitten.

He ran along the corridors of his home as one runs in their backyard. A flood of tears had reached his consciousness, and where for years no moisture had readily touched him, now silent streams were forming and pouring down his face. He climbed the metal bars of the manhole and reached the metal doors leading out to the subway tunnel. With his back pressed up against one of the doors, he forced it open slightly. He listened for trains, then slipped out the openning. He checked carefully in either direction, then made his way to the station.

Both platforms, southbound and northbound, were overcrowded with people waiting for the trains to resume. No trains had passed through the station since he had been followed into the subway tunnel. He stepped up onto the stairs, moved the gate with his bare foot, and stepped onto the platform.

He held the angel carefully, desperately trying to insulate her from the crowds of people bumping into him—some getting off the unmoving train, others trying to get on. At first he tried to slip between people, but he couldn't, there were too many, and they could not see him until he was beside them, and even then there were too many people for anyone to move out of his way. He tried to walk along the edge of the platform, beside the train.

"There he is," he heard someone scream.

He did not look back. He ran along the train and turned into the crowd with the blind rage that made him a force, and he pushed his way through the crowd and up the stairs.

"He has a child," someone screamed.

"Get him," a voice yelled.

"Stop that man," someone else shouted.

He ran to the turnstile, pushed himself through, and once again started jostling with people to get through the crowded Cumberland Terrace.

He dodged around and between people, bumping them in order to get by. He wasn't really sure what he was doing, yet he kept running as fast as he could. Once again people sensed or heard him coming and moved aside, and he passed, for the most part, with relative ease.

He ran first along the corridor and underpasses and back into the mall. Then up the escalator.

* * * * *

Susan sat there at Cafe du Monde and repeated the word again.

"Hope."

It was all she had, she thought. She sat there as if she were in a dream. There were things moving, sounds, smells, and the feel of activity, but it all seemed unreal. She was exhausted and could not sharpen her thoughts or take anything in. She could hear Terence speaking, but his words were distant sounds from some other world. Everything in this world was muffled, blurry, out of focus. No matter what she did, she could not make it any clearer. The world outside had shifted into a peripheral focus.

But then something moved across her field of vision. She lightly slapped herself on the head over and over as if to wake herself from this trance. What was peripheral came back into clear sight. She could not exactly figure out why. She stood up.

"My God . . ." she yelled and screamed incoherently as she started to run.

"I want my mommy," Mei cried.

Susan ran toward the homeless man and her daughter as the man reached Cafe du Monde. He stopped at the counter and spoke to the waiter as if he knew him.

Susan was behind him when he raised the child to the height of the counter and sat her on it.

"This child has lost her mother," he said in a voice that cracked from disuse, pity, and tears.

"I want my mommy," Mei cried again.

The waiter looked at the child.

"Mei," Susan screamed and took her child into her arms as her husband caught up to her.

The homeless man looked at the waiter behind the counter.

"She was lost," he whispered in tears. "Don't know how she got there."

She was wearing his coat and clinging to her mother. She was sobbing and pulled a small kitten from her coat. Her father took it and held it for her as he hugged his daughter and wife.

Two officers quickly stepped up behind the man from the streets and roughly grabbed him.

"Don't bloody well move," one of them warned him as he held a daystick over his head. The other seized his arms to handcuff him.

Terence and Susan hugged and held Mei.

"Is the girl okay?" asked an officer.

"I think so," said Terence, not sure but bursting with joy.

"We'll take her to a hospital, have a doctor look at her," said the officer.

Terence nodded and cried. He held the small, dirty white kitten and hugged and kissed Mei and Susan as best he could.

Mei sobbed. She had been holding back her tears for so long it seemed that her eyes immediately swelled. Tears streamed down her cheeks. She had wanted to cry so many times and had not let herself that now it was her strongest desire, as if these tears would wash away her fears. She was with Mommy and Daddy, who were crying too, and her kitten was okay. She just let the tears continue as she was held, hugged, and kissed.

When her tears eased, she could nod her head when her mommy asked her if she was okay. She reached out to pet her kitten. It was only then she realized she would be in trouble for having the kitten.

"Can I keep it?" she asked her mom.

Susan just hugged her.

"I tried to get the kitten out from the parking garage. We got lost."

"My God . . ." said Susan. "It's okay, Princess."

"You are with us now," said Terence.

"A large cat tried to attack her, but I scared it away."

Terence closed his eyes and put his lips on her forehead.

The police officers grabbed the man from the streets by the arms.

"This way." One of them started leading him toward the exit, to a police car.

Mei kissed her father and reached out for her kitten. When her father moved his head, Mei noticed the man leaving.

"His coat," she said to her mother.

"Wait," said Susan to the police officer escorting the man out. "This is his coat."

She helped Mei take off the large, filthy coat.

The police officer held the man by the arm as another draped the coat over his shoulders.

"Thank you," Mei yelled.

The man bowed and lowered his head.

"He saved us," said Mei to her mother and father.

"He did . . . Of course he did . . ." whispered Susan.

"Wait a minute," Susan said, raising her voice. She stepped toward the police officers. "What are you doing with this man?"

"We're just taking him in for questioning at this point. He has not been charged. He caused quite a disturbance here and in the subway though."

"But he returned our girl," said Terence.

The officer looked at Terence and Susan.

"You can't arrest him," said Susan, "you just can't."

"He'll be okay. We'll just try to find out who he is, and the chief will decide whether or not to press any charges."

"Charges for what?" asked Susan.

"Captain'll decide that, ma'am, once we file a report. Apparently he hurt a woman . . . but we don't think she'll be pressing any charges. We'll take him in. At least he'll get a Christmas dinner out of it, until we charge him or let him go."

"He can have dinner with us," she said. "Surely it's the least we can do for him."

"Ma'am, you'd have to take that up with my captain."

"Can we not speak on his behalf?" asked Terence.

"I can take it up with my captain, sir. That's all I can do. If he were to cause other problems or hurt someone else, we'd be responsible. We'll just check things out before we decide what to do with him."

Mei looked at the man.

"Thank you," she said again.

The man dropped to one knee and lowered his head.

The officer holding him pulled the homeless man to his feet.

"She's an angel . . ." the man whispered.

The officer, Terence, and Susan looked at each other.

"I'll speak to the captain," he said to them.

The homeless man kept his head lowered and started to cry.

He was unable to look at the angel, so he looked at the marble-tiled floor in front of him.

As the officer escorted him toward the exit, he heard the angel say: "Merry Christmas!"

As best he could, he tried to raise his head and look at the ceiling above him, as if her voice had come from there.

Do You Hear What I Hear?

After dinner on Christmas Eve, my grandfather turns off the lights and opens the curtains of his dining room window and waits. His house is built on a hill that overlooks a valley in one direction and the small hamlet of Aarhus in the other. On Christmas Eve, his neighbors harness old Edna and two other horses, put a few bales on the hay wagon, and pick up the neighboring children. At each farmhouse, the children sing Christmas carols and invite everyone to join them as they make their way to Strindberg's Valley, just beyond my grandfather's house. Bob Johnston hangs bells on old Edna, and every Christmas Eve, you can hear those bells ringing throughout the valley.

Christmas is filled with inviting sounds: singing carollers, shared greetings, clinking glasses, the voices of children, crunching snow underfoot, the swoosh of toboggans and skis, the stomping feet of guests dislodging snow on the porch, the howling wind, branches swaying, creaking, Christmas music, logs crackling in the fireplace, and the sound of ringing bells. Bells touch the soul like fire warms the heart. And those bells that Bob Johnston put on old Edna charmed the night air and resonated with such warmth that all in the hamlet listened with reverence. None more than my grandfather.

Ah, but I'm getting ahead of myself, and if Gramps heard me telling you this, he'd be poking my shoulder with his bony finger.

"I've told you a hundred times, don't be spreading things around out of order."

Okay, Gramps, I hear you; so here's the story I named after my grandpa and grandma's favorite Christmas carol.

I guess the first thing I should tell you is that my grandfather is someone I deeply admire. I should honestly confess to loving him more than my own father, even from a young age. We just kind of hit it off, even when I was a child. Gramps is ninety-seven years old now. And although Grandma died over twenty-five years ago, he still lives in the house they shared for forty-seven years, and he would never dream of living anywhere else. And on Christmas Eve, he sets a place for her, sits in the dark, drinks his brandy, eats his turkey dinner, and looks out across Strindberg's Valley at the thousands of Christmas lights.

The Strindberg family started putting up Christmas lights, oh, maybe fifty years ago. At first they put up painted spotlights around some spruce trees in the deep snow at the far end of the valley. Then, as years passed by and the people of Aarhus took to it, they added strings of lights along the creek and the two sides of the valley, near my grandpa's house. Over the years they covered the white birches, red maples, and blue spruce with every color, size, and shape of Christmas light they could lay their hands on.

Almost since the beginning, when there were only a few lights, my grandfather, the Strindbergs, the Johnstons, and others from Aarhus have made a trail each year along the creek.

"Thirty thousand lights in the valley alone," my grandfather tells us when we drive out to see him and the lights before Christmas. Mind you, we haven't gone out to Gramps's place on Christmas Eve since Grandma died; he doesn't take kindly to that. Yet every year my dad attempts to convince Gramps that he should join the family.

"Christmas Eve is for me. Don't be sticking your nose in on it," he says. "Some things just ain't to be shared that way anymore. Understand? Now, be done with this nonsense, for cripes sakes. You should have more sense about you."

Alone, he spends the day of Christmas Eve getting his dinner ready, cooking his small turkey, setting his table, and rubbing his hands together as he continuously fusses over everything. In the late afternoon, he lights a fire, turns out the lights, and quietly sits in his rocking chair until the turkey is ready.

There are probably only two things you shouldn't bother Gramps about:Christmas Eve and Christmas gifts. For my dad's part, I'm not sure if it is the stubbornness between them or what, but every year he buys Gramps a gift and bothers the daylights out of him concerning Christmas Eve.

"What the hell is it with him?" my dad asks us in frustration when we return from visiting and he has tried to convince Gramps to join us for Christmas Eve.

I mean, Gramps spends Christmas Day with us. He always considers it a time for visiting. He just likes to spend Christmas Eve alone. And he doesn't like getting Christmas gifts and gets quite annoyed about it. Never wanted, opened, or used them.

I understood Gramps and always listened to what he said. He was the one person I completely loved when I was growing up. He treated me as a special friend and an equal;something no other adult did. He would remind me to speak louder than the dickens to him, which meant speaking as loud as I could without yelling. So I would sit on his knee, and he'd listen to me, and I'd listen to him. Even when I was getting big, I'd sit on his knee, and he'd smile warmly, never showing that my weight hurt him. After a time, he'd shift and say, "My, but you've grown." When I was not yet a teenager but already quite big, we were both reluctant to give up the idea of me sitting on his knee. It was then I understood that Gramps loved my dad as a son, but he didn't like my dad as a friend; and it was then I understood his affection and love for me.

"Oranges," he said to me one year as he shifted me onto both of his knees, "that's what we'd get for Christmas every year when we was kids. My ma and pa would buy us the biggest navel oranges you ever saw. We had oranges only once a year, Ma and Pa's gift to us. My folks couldn't afford much else, but then, the excitement we'd share over them oranges, well, you'd think they was somethin' magical. We'd sneak up to the trunk Ma kept them in, and we'd sit there and smell them through the wood. Sweetest smell . . .

"It's all I want now that my Anna is no longer with me. I buy myself one navel orange each Christmas. Back then, growing up on a farm in Canada, we didn't see many oranges, but every Christmas morning, we'd all wake up to find one in our stocking. And we could eat them whenever we wanted,had to save the peels, mind you. Ma would use them in cakes 'n pies, tea, and sometimes to make candied fruit pieces too."

Gramps looked sad, and I sat on his knee knowing he was somewhere else . . .

* * * * *

Every Christmas Eve, Pa and Ma would have a big dinner for us. That morning us kids would go out into the yard with Pa to chop the head off the turkey, chase it around till it stopped running, bleed it, then drop the turkey into the hot water, pluck, and clean it. Afterwards, we'd proudly bring it in to Ma, who'd do all the fussing. The whole day was spent in preparation for the Christmas dinner. And when dinner was ready in the evening, we'd sit around the table and hold hands for a couple of moments. We'd sit with our thoughts, our wishes, and our love for Ma and Pa. Then Ma would break the silence. "Let us give thanks," she would say, and we'd raise our heads mighty high. "Once again, Magnus, on behalf of my good family and ever-loving husband, we send you and Florence heartfelt thanks for the turkey we are about to receive. Thank you, Magnus."

"Amen," Pa would say.

"Amen," us kids would repeat.

My ma's brother, Magnus, worked for a butcher in town, and he didn't make much money, but every year a farmer gave him a live turkey, and every year he'd give it to his sister Kay, my ma. They would join us some years, but usually they took to caring for our Aunt Florence's mother.

We were called godless folk by the townspeople back then 'cause we never went to church. We knew no God, but every Christmas Eve we prayed to thank Uncle Magnus. "Backward, godless people" we was called, and it was true, but there was self-righteous fear in those words from the folks in town, and we thanked Ma and Pa that we didn't go there much. We worked hard to get by as best we could on our farm, that's all. Those first years was a struggle never mentioned. And us kids sure looked forward to Uncle Magnus and Aunt Florence visiting us,it was like taking a vacation when they arrived. Ma and Pa was so happy, and Uncle Magnus would play with us for hours, as if he was one of us kids. They had no kids themselvesóAunt Florence couldn't, and Uncle Magnus stood by her whenever he saw her looking upon us with a personal longing. At such times, my younger brother Peter would tell Ma that he'd go live with them, and Ma would give him a stern look so as he'd keep his tongue from wagging. But Uncle Magnus would smile without taking offence, and he'd grab hold of his wife's hand and kiss her gently. He and Aunt Florence were godless folks too. I think that's why we liked them and prayed to them at Christmas.

Then came the war. I was of age when that warm August of 1914 seemed to dry out our land, and we could only hope for rain. Pa came home from town one day with a week-old newspaper. He showed me the advertisement for recruiting.

"It's your choice, son," he said to me, "but give her some thought."

Everything we did was our choice.

"What ought we to?" we'd ask him.

"To make your minds determined," he'd say.

And that's as close as he ever ventured to telling us what to do. With the advertisement in the paper, he was asking me to consider something that was impossible for me to conceive.

But I waited for dinner, 'cause the dinner table was where we held our family discussions.

"Whaddya think about this here war?" I asked Ma and Pa as we started to eat.

"It's gotta be your choice, son," Pa said.

"I know, Pa," I said, "but whaddya think about it?"

"Well now, son, Canada's a good country, a free country worth fightin' for. They don't know no capital tax, no stealing crops. Now, if they see fit to tax us like other places, well then, I see fit to think otherwise, 'cause then it's a different story, you understand."

"They say it'll be over before Christmas, son," continued Ma, "so you don't have to miss our turkey dinner or nothin' like that, and they don't pay none too bad, which helps out. It looks like it may be a hard winter comin' ahead."

"I'll decide by morning and let you know," I said.

My parents were godless people, and I was proud of them for that. In many ways they prepared me for the future, but nothing they did prepared me for the army. I ended up in the doghouse on the second day I arrived in England, and six years later, when I returned home, I was still in the same doghouse. I spent over five years peeling tubers, washing, scrubbing, boiling, mashing, and in the end smelling like a tuber. No question about her, I was the best tuber peeler in the entire Canadian regiment. When I joined, I was put on a train to Halifax, Nova Scotia, and from there, within a month, I was shipped to England and had no sooner arrived when they had us marching through drills and digging ditches. I'd no sooner finished digging a ditch when I'd be told to fill her back in. I'd never run into such nonsense in anything I'd partook.

"Why, sir?" I asked.

"Because I said so," I was told.

"Not good enough, sir," I said.

"How about this?" asked my drill sergeant as he socked me in the side of the head with the back of his hand.

"No, sir," I said as I regained my balance and threw down my spade.

The sergeant picked up the shovel and tried to bat me with

it. I grabbed the spade as it was about to say hello to the side of my face. I took it from him and cracked it in two over my knee. He looked at me and backed away. And I knew then and there that I'd have been better to crack him in two over my knee and be done with him.

"You'll peel tubers for the rest of your days if it's the last thing I do," he yelled and kicked dirt in my direction as he stormed off. He held true to his word; I peeled tubers for five years.

A lot of men died in that war, a lot of good men. I'm sure I peeled tubers for most of them on our side, especially the ones at Ypres. I was not often close to the battle lines. I was usually behind, doing my duty.

In October of 1914, thirty-three thousand of us Canadians was volunteers for overseas service. We was to finish our trainin' in England, and we was ready by the spring of 1915, in time to see action at the Second Battle of Ypres. Right at first, we was just battalions within British formations, and that was just as well with most of the boys and me; that way they couldn't be sending us all in to be killed at once. But the politicians, with country pride and all, wanted us put together as the First and Second Divisions, and we was headed by Lieutenant-Commander Arthur Currie. He was a good man. But at Ypres, our side lost over a hundred thousand men in the first two battles. Red rivers and muddy lakes of blood. Humans, you understand, doing this to each other. Then, there was the third week in April, a week I'll never forget; the Germans shot out cylinders of chlorine gas;the agonized frenzy of the men in them trenches is branded in my memory like living scar tissue. But our troops on the flank of the breach stood firm, and with English and Indian reinforcements, we held with only a slight withdrawal . . .

For over three more years I was behind those lines in the mud of Flanders. It was behind mounds of mud and human flesh that I learned for myself what Ma and Pa took for granted: When I saw so many young men die so senselessly for land to be taken, lost, retaken, and relost, and when I looked around at the trenches and the thousands of young men creating battle lines in mud, I knew there was no God.

And it was behind those lines that I was hit. With peeling tubers all day, I took to the fine art of conversation. In my whole life, I have loved nothing more than conversing with people. In the end, I'd have to admit that I loved to argue and debate as much as anybody and probably a hoot more than most. It was like I couldn't get enough of the human voice, and I never exhausted myself with discussions. When you're peeling tubers, nothing passes the time of day better. I developed quite a reputation for it. "You should be a barrister or politician," the fellows would say to me. I tried to be friendly to all the boys so they'd know some joy in Flanders. The boys liked me . . . then our back lines was hit. I'd been talking so much I didn't hear a thing till a shell exploded into one of the sinks beside me, maybe ten feet away. The impact wrecked my shoulder and blew out my eardrums, damaging one drum totally and leaving me nearly deaf. It was waking up the next day in that there British hospital tent, in December of 1918, when I realized with certainty how much hearing another's voice had meant to me. But I heard no other voice nor anything else. So, like the others who survived the war, we missed one more Christmas before we slowly made our way back home to a world tired of war and a world quickly changing,and many of us with scars that never healed.

That Christmas, lying in bed in a makeshift hospital tent, a small parcel arrived. It was a gift from Ma and Pa. Somehow they had managed to get me the largest navel orange I'd ever seen . . .

Each year I carry on the Christmas of my ma and pa. My godless folks had a Christmas tradition that I was rightfully proud of, and to this day, I carry it on in my life, for as Pa would say, "It's your choice, son."

As far as concerns war, I say this: Reason with me, talk, scream, or yell, but don't use no shovel, stick, or gun. I am a man; treat me as one. I can think; take me or leave me as such. I come made no other way. That's what my folks taught me, and I'm mighty proud of my lesson learned.

* * * * *

My grandfather patted my shoulder and put me down off his knee.

"Run along now. I need to be by myself for a spell. Maybe this year you'll join me for a Christmas Eve and share a part of my ma and pa's Christmas. But run along now, and don't be telling this here to your father, for cripes sake. That's all I'd be needin'."

I left my grandfather there in his chair and slowly walked outside toward the barn.

When I told Dad Gramps wanted me to join him for Christmas Eve, I thought he would be upset. He wasn't. Just smiled and patted my head.

"Your grandfather sure has a spot for you."

The day of Christmas Eve, late in the afternoon, Dad drove me to Gramps's house.

"We'll pick you both up in the morning," he said. "Don't be drinking too much brandy."

"I won't, Dad," I said.

I walked to the side entrance and saw Gramps standing outside at the edge of the valley that extended beyond his farm. In his heavy winter overcoat, he looked rather frail standing there in the cold with the wind blowing him and the snow toward the hill. For a moment I thought the wind may just blow him away.

"Grandpa," I yelled so that I wouldn't give him a fright.

He didn't hear me.

He stood at the edge of the valley, looking out over it. Normally, he liked to walk through the valley, especially at night when the Christmas lights were on, and he would join others in the carolling. But this year he had taken a couple of falls, which left his legs rather weak and numb.

"Grandpa," I repeated, but not as loud because I was getting closer to him.

It was an oddity with Gramps that you had to raise your voice to a yell for him to hear you, but you had better make it appear as if you were speaking in a normal voice and never in anger. He didn't take kindly to that, and he'd let you know in one jumping-leap-of-a-hurry. It was a fine line, and he picked up on it quickly. "No need to scream in anger. Trying to deafen and offend those with proper senses?" he'd ask.

"Grandpa," I said one more time.

He slowly turned toward me. He smiled and his cheeks were red, but he looked sad.

"The snow is pretty deep," I said, as if explaining to him why he couldn't go.

He didn't respond. We stood there looking out over the valley. He turned and looked at me for a moment, then we made our way inside.

He had spent the day preparing a small turkey. When he opened the door, the whole house was filled with aromas of turkey, sweet cranberry relish, baked yams, and rum sauce for the Christmas pudding. The fire was crackling, and the flames cast beautiful shadows across his living room.

"Mind ya to wipe your feet," he said.

Then he turned to me, took my coat, and placed it on a hook, hanging his beside it.

"Bit of daylight yet," he said to me, which meant we weren't yet to sit at the table in front of the large windows in the dining room.

He opened the brandy, poured us both some, then turned to the fire and sat in front of it, waving at me to do the same. I pulled up a chair and quietly sat, watching the fire and watching Gramps in his rocking chair. In the silence of the late afternoon, his home quickly turned to evening, with the sky growing dark and the house taking on the orange-yellow glow of the fire.

"It's time," he said.

We rose and made our way to the dining room. He lit the

candles, slowly carved the turkey, and asked me to pour him more brandy. We sat and raised our heads in silence for a moment. And I couldn't help it, I sadly looked over at the empty place setting.

Gramps slowly raised his glass.

"A toast," he said. "A toast to my Anna, my pa, my ma, and my Aunt Florence and Uncle Magnus. Merry Christmas to you and much thanks. You are the people I've most respected and loved."

He looked at me and smiled a sad smile, then raised his glass and touched mine. We drank and started dinner.

Each time he raised his glass, he looked over at the empty place setting, as if to let Grandma know it was okay, that she was not forgotten. And each time our glasses touched, he'd ask me to describe what I heard. I'd tell him what the ring of the crystal was like, and tears would well up in his eyes.

When dinner was finished, he blew out the candles, and we sat at the table in front of the large windows. The Christmas lights from the valley glittered all around the room. He nodded his head gently and sipped his brandy. After a while, he asked me about the sounds of the evening: the wind, the creaking floorboards, the crackling fire. I knew his questions were in anticipation of what he really wanted to hear: Edna's bells as the horses slowly trotted their way to the valley, pulling the wagon of children. We were silent for a moment, then, faintly at first and growing louder, I heard the bells and made every effort I could to give my words the sound of those bells as their ringing filled the valley around us. As I spoke, he sat still, leaning toward the window. He squinted his eyes like he was looking into the night and seeing the sound of those bells. Often I was sure he was hearing them better than me, like he had extra senses when the sky was dark and it was Christmas Eve. The ring seemed to carry on the wind, and he gently tapped his chest as if he felt the sound there.

As the hay wagon drew nearer, we rose and stepped outside to the edge of the valley, where he had stood in the afternoon.

The wagon stopped below, and the children came toward us and sang. He stood and stared at them with tears in his eyes. By reading their lips, he knew they were singing his and Grandma's favorite Christmas carol. After finishing, they waved a Merry Christmas to us and rejoined their parents, who had stayed by the wagon at the creek. Gramps stood there for a very long time before I coaxed him to move. When he finally turned away, he very slowly went inside and sat by the window overlooking the valley of Christmas lights. Tremulously, he started humming the Christmas carol he had not heard.

When he finished, he stood up and walked over to the Christmas tree in the corner. From a stocking hanging down from one of the branches, he took out the two largest navel oranges I've ever seen. He put one by the empty place setting on the dining room table, and the other he gave to me.

"Merry Christmas, my boy," he said as he handed me the orange.

He put his hand on my shoulder, and together we looked out the window at the valley of Christmas lights.

And as the bells on Edna faded along the hills of the valley, I leaned toward him and whispered, "Merry Christmas, Gramps."

A Grey Christmas

"Traffic."

I tap my fingers on the wheel with one hand and rub my forehead with the other.

It's dark outside and raining. It seems too cold to rain, yet the rain beats down in endless waves, tapping on the roof and hood of my car. I'm stuck in highway traffic heading north of the city. My home town is an hour's drive from here. At this rate it will take me two. Visiting hours are till seven.

"They will probably let you stay longer if he's not sleeping—and if you're nice," my mom had said to me on the phone. She stressed the word nice as if it were something unknown to me. "I told them you would be there around five."

It is already five-thirty. I've barely moved in the last twenty minutes.

I promised to spend at least a couple of hours with Dad on Christmas Eve—my bargain with Mom for her to feel okay about visiting her oldest sister, who has taken ill.

The road is wet and is lit by the endless brake lights in front of me. The traffic is fine in the other direction, though, should I change my mind and just go home. I feel like it. It's been a lousy day. I was hoping to get away early enough to see our old house, which Mom sold in the spring . . . but I'll be short on time now and lucky to see Dad.

Where are all these people going? It amazes me how many people are on the road at a time like this. I honked the horn like a madman when I first got on the highway—I mean, I hate not moving—but I calmed down eventually and even let a couple of cars squeeze in front of me. After all, it is Christmas Eve.

I'm just hoping to get there soon. I already feel bad about being late.

It's not easy for me to understand the feelings I have toward Dad. And now with children of my own, I feel kind of guilty. Life is hectic. Then children show up at the door, and suddenly time's what everyone else has. We have two children. How the hell did my parents have nine? How could anyone keep their senses?

I grew up convinced I was so different from my parents. Yet I remember being in the car with Dad, and he'd be thinking over mumbled thoughts, tapping his fingers on the steering wheel with one hand while he rubbed his forehead with the other, just like I do. And I snapped this afternoon . . . just like Dad. I swore I never would . . . I can remember my thoughts when Dad would lose it. I saw the same look of horror on the faces of my kids, Karitsa and Sal.

This afternoon we had gotten a Christmas tree, and we were doing some shopping when I lost it. When they were in the car afterward, and I looked over my shoulder into the back seat, it was anger, hurt, and shock I saw on their faces. It could have been me in that back seat looking at Dad. This was the first year I left so much to do till the last minute. It was raining then as it is now, and someone had stolen our Christmas tree.

"Are you two okay?" I tried to ask them calmly, as if nothing had happened.

They had seemed so happy coming with me to pick out a Christmas tree.

"Are you two okay?" I asked again, looking over my shoulder.

They were not okay. How could they be? An alien from some other planet had just dragged them across the floor of a busy shopping mall. They had whined, cried, and gone silent.

We had spent half an hour picking out a Christmas tree we all liked and tying it to the top of the station wagon. Except, because it had been so busy at the cash register, it had taken us almost another hour before we paid for it and got out of the parking lot. Then it started to rain. We raced to the mall only to have to drive around for over thirty-five minutes to find a place to park. I should have just parked on the grass like everyone else, but I was trying to set an example. Then we fought crowds to get in and fought crowds to get from store to store. We seemed to walk around forever. All of us were tired.

I stopped at one shop that sold speciality dishes. I knew Tana would love them. The dishes were ivory bone china decorated with hand-painted green leaves and lines of gold.

Even then, Karitsa and Sal were tugging at my arm: "Come on, Dad, let's go home."

But I stood there doing that half-paying-attention half-ignoring- them thing my parents used to do that drove me crazy. I continued looking at the dishes in the window.

"Wait here. I'll just be a minute," I said.

"Aw, Dad . . ."

I stepped inside. I'm not sure how long I looked around, but when I came out, they were gone.

I simply went blank. I thought I was dreaming . . . I didn't see a sign of them. I could feel myself go weak at the knees.

The mall has two levels of numerous shops between two large department stores. I looked toward the stores on either side, then at the stairs in one direction and the escalators in the other. There were bodies and heads in a walking, shifting flow, as if the mass actually moved and swayed together to block my line of sight. I quickly stepped toward the railing and looked down to the lower level. The mall was too crowded to see anyone in particular. I turned in each direction . . . and something in the corner of my eye caught my attention. I thought I saw a head of hair I recognized in the Disney Store. They were walking toward a large television screen at the back.

"Jesus Christ," I cursed under my breath.

But I felt this tremendous weight lifted from my shoulders. I calmly walked up to them and sternly said, "I thought we agreed you would wait for me, Karitsa, Sal." They stopped like they had been caught stealing. "When I tell you to wait, you must wait. Let's go."

I marched them out of the store as if I were my dad ready to box their ears.

Then it was the coat store.

"We want to go home," Sal said.

Good coats cost a fortune. That's fine if you have a fortune to spend, but I didn't. Besides, my wife is the breadwinner in our home; she would kill me if I spent that kind of money on her. So I got us out of that store in a reasonable hurry. Then I saw a lovely dress in the window of a women's clothing store. I thought it would look good on Tana. It was a little more than I hoped to spend, but close enough. By this time I was probably more tired than my little guys. I grabbed one of the dresses off the rack.

"I'll take this," I said to a lady beside me.

She looked at me like she was about to tell me what I could do with the dress. I guess she didn't work there. Before the woman decided to assault me, I made my way to the line at the cash register. I don't know how long it took by the time I paid for it and got it wrapped. I tucked the gift-wrapped box under my arm and led my little guys toward the stairs.

"Come on," I tried to encourage them, "just one more stop. We're almost finished. Then we'll get you an ice cream."

They looked tired and bored.

I led them down the stairs toward the lingerie store. I always buy Tana lingerie. I had wanted to buy her some perfume too, but I had pretty much spent the limit. At the lingerie store Sal started complaining again, but Karitsa saw some hats and with bright eyes turned toward them.

"Don't leave the store," I told them.

I looked around . . . and when I looked back, Karitsa was trying on a hat. She stood in front of the mirror and flipped the brim up and then down. She called Sal over, and he reluctantly joined her.

I continued looking. As I walked to the back of the store, I felt strange all of a sudden, as if I had waited too long to eat. Then there was this woman I became aware of. I could only see the profile of her face, but it made me feel odd and lightheaded. The room swayed. I rubbed my eyes and the back of my neck. I know it sounds crazy, but I felt like I was in a trance and sort of followed this woman around the store. She reminded me of someone from my first day at high school. A woman who worked in the office at school had causally brushed her dress against me, and it had filled me with a kind of excitement that lasted till I was in my teens. It was a silk dress, soft and cool. Each time I remember her, I can smell the scent of her perfume. She had long, sandy-brown hair, a beautiful face . . . The feel of her dress had sensually swept across me, and I think at that moment, I became aware of what it meant to be a sexual being. I had wanted to touch her, right there, and I almost did. I got out of the office in a hell of a hurry. I mean, I really felt I would do something I shouldn't, and I had no control over it. Now, I looked at this woman in the lingerie store and felt a bit of the same.

She politely smiled . . .

"May I help you, sir?" a saleswoman asked.

I hadn't seen her standing beside me.

"No," I said, "no, I'm just looking."

And I looked at this other woman in the store, and I had tears in my eyes. I thought I might cry. Sometimes a melancholy feeling creeps up on me and caress my throat. I can barely speak. A woman can just walk by, and something in me reacts . . . like I'm missing something . . .

I felt such a longing . . . I wanted to sit down and think, but there was no chair nearby. So I closed my eyes for a moment, took slow deep breaths to calm myself, and turned the other way.

There she was. She was holding a sleek, burgundy-colored gown that would melt me. I watched her walk toward an open armoire filled with drawers of nylons. She stopped, turned, and looked at me. She seemed to hold that look for a moment before she turned the other way. I stood there, staring at her; there seemed to be no one else in the store. There was a warm fuzziness of pleasure in the thought that perhaps I would speak to her. I would be bold. As I drew closer to her, I wanted to say something, but I didn't know what the hell to say. "Nice day," I whispered to myself as if to practise. I can be such a fool. Besides, it was an ugly day.

She casually turned, picked up a lovely satin nightshirt, and tried to find a mirror. She pressed it against herself and moved her head first this way, then that. I was filled with this incredible urge to tell her I was taken with her . . . but I didn't say anything as she passed near me to make her way toward the dressing room. I did follow her, though, thinking I might get a chance to say something. Again she seemed to look in my direction, but she clearly looked past me. She was oblivious to it all, I guess: my presence, her beauty—its effect on me . . . Why did so many beautiful women make me feel this way? And this feeling always reminded me of another woman . . . I had met . . .

"Ah . . . Jesus Christ . . ."

What can I say?

I try not to think of it much anymore.

"Where's Karitsa and Sal?" a voice inside of me asked.

I looked in the direction of the front of the store.

They were gone.

"Son of a bitch," I cursed.

Having lost and found them once already, I didn't worry for them so much as get angry. My temper just hit the roof. I ground my teeth together and cursed again as I walked to the front of the store.

"Goddamnit . . ."

For the first time, I had serious thoughts of spanking them despite our agreement to never hit our children.

I squeezed the gift-wrapped box and quickly walked out into the mall. I turned from one direction to the other as people walked by me. I didn't see them. In anger I started walking. I barged between two people and bumped into someone else who told me to be careful. I ran upstairs toward the Disney Store and bumped into an old couple and didn't apologize. I ran past the girl greeting everyone at the door and quickly looked toward the large television screen in the back.

They were not there.

I ran out of the store and approached the railing to look down to the lower level. There were people everywhere, and the hustle and bustle of voices seemed to be rising. There was the echo of Christmas carols being sung somewhere. There was a kind of sweetness in the air that I could smell, and it was mixed with the scent of perfume, soap, and coffee. I had always wanted to develop a policy for this kind of situation, but they seemed so young.

"Damn it all!"

They could be anywhere, I thought.

I panicked.

"The car," a voice in my head told me.

I started running toward the exit and the parking lot. I ran into several people. I knocked an entire rack of dresses and blouses over outside a store. I just kept running toward the exit and then headed for the car.

I got outside and stopped. "You stupid idiot!" I screamed as loud as I could at myself.

Only then did I realize they would have no idea where the car was.

I rushed back inside and returned to the store where I had lost them. I yelled at a clerk, asking if she had seen them. She hadn't.

"Check with the people at the info centre, right there," she said, pointing out the doorway and trying to answer calmly.

I went to the counter and nervously spoke. A woman announced their names; we waited. They didn't come.

"If they show up, just call for me," I yelled.

I couldn't wait.

I ran along a row of shops, looking from window to window, calling their names aloud. I ran along the lower level from store to store, then went upstairs to the upper level. I approached each store with growing anger. I looked constantly over the handrail to see if I might spot them on the lower level.

"Goddamn you!" I screamed at myself and had the delightful experience of everyone turning and looking at me as if I were mad. In some kind of newly discovered frustration, I threw my gift-wrapped box violently to the floor and kicked it.

Then I saw them. They were at the front of the line to get a bag of candy from Santa in his large Village House.

I clenched my teeth together so hard they hurt. I grabbed the gift-wrapped box and stormed down the escalator, stepped over into the exit path between some children, and walked up the ramp as Santa placed both of them comfortably on his knee.

"And what would you two like for—"

"Jesus Christ!" I yelled and grabbed both of them violently by the arms.

Then, gripping them tightly, I marched forward while they desperately tried to keep up. Despite their stumbling along behind me, after a short distance they both gave up pleading that I was hurting them, and they cried to no effect as I dragged them toward the car. At the car, I opened the back door and placed them roughly into the back seat. It was at this precise moment that I noticed someone had stolen the Christmas tree—bungi cords included—off the roof of the car.

"Goddamn it!" I screamed and pounded the car roof with my open hand.

I opened the car door, got in, and slammed it as hard as I could.

"Shit!" I screamed.

Then I sat there trying to take deep breaths to calm myself.

My children had never seen me like this. I had never seen me like this.

"They are safe," I tried to tell myself.

I would never have forgiven myself for such carelessness if anything had happened.

I was madder than hell . . . and we still didn't have a Christmas tree.

I sat there in silence. I remembered my dad, and how so often my brother and I waited in the car for him. Dad would borrow a car on the weekend from his brother or my mother's best friend, and we would just go along for the ride while he went into one place after another to do his errands. I remember the first time I heard any swear words. My younger brother and I were sitting alone in the car; he was pretending to drive, and I was telling him to honk the horn and watch out for the oncoming truck. Dad returned from having a quick beer at the Legion.

"Goddamn assholes . . ." he said.

My brother and I looked at each other. We weren't sure what any of it meant, but it didn't sound good. We figured these were bad words of some sort. We sunk a little lower in our seats, and I could see Dad looking over at us to see if we had noticed. He was rather quiet after returning from the next stop.

Today you can't leave your children in the car. Someone may take them, beat them, do . . . who the hell knows what in the few moments you think you may be gone . . .

I sat there in the car, breathing heavily, trying to recover, and trying to figure out why I had gotten like this. It was strange to think the world was so different from when Dad had raised us, but we were more alike than I ever cared to admit.

I drove in silence, picked up another tree, and took our guys home. They too were quiet. It was a sombre group returning home to celebrate that we had gotten our Christmas tree.

Only after a late lunch and with the building excitement of Christmas Eve did our guys become friendly with me at all.

"You have to go?" Karitsa asked after quite some time, still with some residual hurt and shock.

She was a sensitive child, but a determined one. Yet how could I explain such choices to a six-year-old? I could only say, "I have to go and see Grandpa. He's not well."

How many times had I made choices I wasn't readily able

to explain to our guys? A lot it seemed. But Karitsa always seemed to be confidently standing there wanting to know. I found it difficult to explain that I had to go because a part of me felt guilty about my father for reasons unknown. She was always so intense when she asked such questions, always so focused. I found it hopeless to answer when she gazed up at me that way. Sometimes she looked right at me, as if she were the adult. Frankly, I'm not totally at ease with her knowing me that way. I love my parents, but they were parents. Karitsa looks at me as if she expects to someday be my best friend. It scares the bejesus out of me. Tana was carrying her. . . ahhh . . . feel like hell about it . . . It was a Christmas Eve, and Tana was eight months pregnant. A girl took me by the hand, and I let her . . . like a little boy . . .

It bothers me . . . I don't like thinking about it . . . I try to hold down that side of me. So when my daughter intently looks at me with her hazelish-grey-brown eyes, I feel ashamed. Her voice haunts me. It says, "I don't trust you. Who really knows you if the people you love don't?"

"But why tonight, Daddy?" she had asked. "It's Christmas Eve. The tree is not finished, and you have to read us a story."

I didn't know what to say. I was never strong enough to offer an explanation to her when I felt like this. I didn't know where to begin. In her presence, my heart melts, and tears well up in my eyes.

There are so many images, memories really, that form an endless sequence of film footage, like a reel of disjointed flashes from my past. I regret things, like stealing candy when I was young. But there is one regret that lingers on and on. As a young man, sleeping with someone became a hunger that grew. I always thought I would satiate it; I haven't. When I married, I just refused to take any steps in that direction. Yet this hunger never seems to rest. I don't actively pursue it, but I know I would actively accept it, even today . . . as I did as an expecting father on a Christmas Eve long ago . . . before Karitsa was born. I know it doesn't make me a monster, but there is a grey area, a rainy drizzle I wanted to avoid. It always got in the way . . . if you asked me, I would say that it's not enough to avoid the bad, the pathetic, the mistaken, the ugly. There is something worse and more likely for me . . .

"Ah, Daddy, have Christmas with us."

She is such a happy child. Often I just stare at her. She has sensitive eyes and an alert, inquisitive mind . . . sometimes it's all I can do to not cry when I look at her.

"Mommy," she said, raising her voice to get Tana's attention in the kitchen. "Mommy, Daddy's gone far away, and he won't come back."

She is such a lovely child. She's six years old, has light brown hair, a warm smile, and is wearing one of her favourite hats. I buy hats for her. I love to see her take a hat and immediately know which way to wear it, bend it, shape it, angle it. She wears hats sideways, backward, tipped up, down, and any which way except the way I intuitively expect it to be worn. Her big, hazelish-grey-brown eyes beamed out from beneath them . . .

"Mommy, he won't come back, he's still gone far away. Make him come back, Mommy," she said.

I looked down at her and then over at Sal as he came into the room. He is two years younger than Karitsa.

"Hot chocolate's almost ready," he announced.

Sal has dark brown hair and dark brown eyes. And for his birthday this past summer we bought him denim coveralls. He hasn't worn anything else since. He is a quiet boy, very serious, and he watches and listens to everything as if he will remember it for the rest of his life. Often it seems like a threat.

When Tana came into the living room with hot chocolate, we all sat on the floor in front of the couch, facing the fireplace. Karitsa was dressed in my denim shirt, and she had rolled up the sleeves until the arms looked like pant legs. One night she asked me if she could use my jean shirt as a nightshirt "Cause it would be warm, Dad." She wears a little brocaded tee shirt underneath it and some socks. It's her pyjamas. Sal was sitting still, waiting for me to speak so that he might remember it for the rest of his life.

I knew I had to leave soon. I tried to remember if I looked at my dad the way these guys look at me.

"Mommy, make him come back," said Karitsa. "He's gone away."

"He's thinking about his father," said Tana. "Give him a few moments, and he'll be back to join us for a short while before he has to go."

"Why does he have to go, Mom?"

"To see Grandpa, you know that. Grandpa's not doing so well."

That seemed to cast a silence on them, and they sat staring at the crackling fire as it cast the room in yellows and oranges.

"Grandpa's sick," said Sal after a while.

"Yes, he is," said Tana.

I sat there looking at my family . . . and then I couldn't help but think that maybe if they knew everything, they would feel toward me what I often felt toward Dad. It's a sad thought . . . even though I love him. Karitsa and Sal never really knew my dad. Their grandpa is someone they really don't understand. He was kind of losing it even when they were younger. For me there are so many things to remember. Some good, some not so good. But now he has gotten quite old . . . and he has Alzheimer's. He's a mystery to Karitsa and Sal, someone to make fun of the way children will when they don't understand. Yet he is to me what I am to these guys. It's odd to be a parent. We just seem to be struggling along, growing up, then suddenly we're adults—husband, wife, father, mother . . . I just wonder if our kids feel about me the way I feel and felt about Dad, even at their age.

Tana put her arm around me and handed me a cup of hot chocolate.

"Daddy, are you going to drink your hot chocolate?" asked Sal.

I turned to face Sal and pulled him up onto my knee.

Why does it feel so good to have them on your knee? I remember sitting on Dad's knee . . . feeling his scruffy unshaven face when he kissed me and tied my shoes. He always liked it when we sat on his knee. I remember how Dad often tasted of aftershave and sometimes beer. I kiss my son too, and put my hand on his head, and stroke his hair, much like Dad did to me.

I kissed Sal's cheek.

"Hey, Dad's back," said Karitsa.

"Yeah," said Sal, "maybe it will snow now."

"Just in time for Christmas," said Karitsa. "You know how Grandpa loved a white Christmas."

Tana got up and came over to kiss me.

"The fire's warm, Daddy," said Sal.

"Do you have to go, Dad? Couldn't you go tomorrow and take us with you?" asked Karitsa.

I looked at her. She breaks my heart.

"Your dad must be with his father tonight—Grandpa's not well," said Tana.

I patted Karitsa's shoulder.

When these guys were born, I started writing children's stories that we would read on Christmas Eve. As Karitsa and Sal grew, it became one of their favourite parts of Christmas Eve. We will be doing that on Christmas Day this year instead.

* * * * *

The traffic is still heavy, but finally moving.

There's an accident in the right two lanes ahead of me. Cars facing the wrong direction, smashed into one another, debris on the road, and glass shattered everywhere across the pavement. One of the cars is so badly smashed that there is no way anyone could have survived.

"Jesus . . ."

A child's car seat is dangling out of the space that was once the back window . . .

"Christ . . ."

I guess the ambulances have already taken away the injured. The tow trucks are removing the smashed cars. A woman is sitting on the side of the road with her head on her knees, her hand over her face. An officer is talking to her. Beside her, there is a car door that is folded in half. I guess it was removed from the car with a saw. I can see the cut along one side of it.

"My God . . ."

I hate that stuff, hate seeing it . . . hate thinking about it. I have the world's weakest stomach . . . next to my mom . . .

Once by the accident, I step on the gas and focus intently on the road in front of me. I want to get there before I'm too late to see Dad at all.

* * * * *

I often wonder how well I really know Dad.

He loved many things in life, although one of those things was beer. But it wasn't till we were older that it became a problem. None of us likes to say Dad had a drinking problem . . . was an alcoholic. And maybe it wasn't so much a problem as it was a mystery; it was just so difficult to understand. Maybe life got too complicated for him. It's difficult to know your father when you are nothing but a son. Not a friend. Not a confidant. Not even someone to talk to. It wasn't that I tried to be more, it was just that I didn't once question or try to change the nature of our relationship. Not once.

As an adult with children, I can see how Dad reached out to us, but for the life of me, I never saw it as a child. Even when it was obvious, even when there was nothing else to account for what Dad was trying to do or say. Why was I so stupid with my own father? Dad sought what any father sought from any son or daughter.

"I just must have been stupidly blind . . ."

I remember mornings, when the house was quiet; the

world seemed to slow down, and everybody else slept. I would get up with Dad as he got ready for work. I liked getting up early . . . still do. On weekends we would go out into the yard . . .

Dad was a simple man. He loved gardening; plants and flowers had a special place in his heart. When we were young, a garden was a necessity for a large family. Dad insisted that flowers were too, and he planted rows and rows of them in the garden, around the house, and anywhere else for that matter. I don't know how many times I was on my hands and knees with Dad as he showed me various flowers, how to plant seeds, care for shrubs and bulbs.

"Smell the earth," he would say. He would take hold of some soil in his hands and bring it to his nose. "Nothing quite like it; a clean, just-rained smell."

I would smell the earth in his hands.

"Put a little on your tongue, just to taste it," he said. "Don't chew it, just move it around a bit and spit it out. Tastes like good soil, doesn't it? That's what a garden carrot tastes like."

Dad's sensitive touch with plants and flowers extended to his palate for food. He loved picking something fresh and cooking it. And although he didn't fish, he loved to cook it. Our Uncle Magnus and Aunt Florence would send us sturgeon from the northern lakes that were longer than our kitchen table. Dad would barbecue them and send me off to the hillside of the field next door to pick wild asparagus. He'd fry the spears in butter and garlic and pour them over the barbecued fish. Wow . . . was it good. Other times we would go into the woods to find morels to fry in butter. Later it would be puff-balls that we'd pick from around the high school football field. He was never too sure about which mushrooms were edible, so we usually left them alone. And when everyone else was away, he would buy some strong cheese, and we would sit in the back yard and have cheese with fresh squid or clams. Sometimes friends or relatives would go fishing and give us trout, bass, perch, pickerel, and even catfish, or in the early spring, smelts.

We would help clean them out back on the picnic table, which was covered with newspaper. Sometimes I would follow him into the basement, and he would open some blue cheese or Stilton, and occasionally some Limburger cheese. The house smelled like hell for the rest of the day, but I'd sit on his knee, and he would give me some and let me finish the remaining beer in his bottle.

Dad loved beer. There was no getting around it. He drank too much, too often. But even as a child he taught me the pleasure of beer—much in the same way I try to show our children the pleasure of wine. And as a child, I hated the arguments in the house because of drink, but the arguments were few and far between. Dad was usually a quiet, gentle man who enjoyed the simple pleasures in life, even when life got hectic.

I'm not sure how old I was when I first saw Dad leave the house without kissing Mom. Maybe ten—I don't know. Dad considered it as ungentlemanly as dining without a shirt, not shaving before going to bed, walking with your hands in your pockets, or raising your voice when talking to a woman. I remember profoundly the look of boyish hurt on his face when he left the house out of anger without kissing Mom. That look sticks in my mind—I never leave the house without kissing Tana, no matter how pissed I am. Dad kissing Mom is probably the clearest memory I have of both of my parents. Dad wouldn't venture to the back yard without first kissing Mom good-bye. They both had a cute way about them when they kissed. They held their lips tightly together, pursed out, as if they were children stealing a moment of pleasure.

I remember the good times, the times of love and tranquillity, and the times of turmoil as well. And all of it came wrapped together as one large package every Christmas Eve.

Christmas was often a time of overindulgence, and Dad was not adverse to it. When we were younger, I think there was a lot of lightness and humour in his questionable state. But as we grew older, the lightness and humour seemed to sour and grow into a bitterness. The bitterness was so out of character for him. It's what really convinces me that none of us understood Dad, not as a man. We were only able to know him as a father, a provider. I wish I would have added a few more smiles to his life . . . a few more laughs . . . my sisters did . . . he had such a nice smile for them . . . such a boyish giggle . . . such a special place in his heart . . .

Ah . . . there's the town limits and the population sign that hasn't been changed in fifty years.

I always have to take a few deep breaths when I'm coming back into town, so excuse me for a moment while I hold one till I get to the stoplights.

* * * * *

"Ahhh . . . that's better."

My home town has a kind of strip where everyone cruised up and down the street with friends to see what was happening. I drive rather quickly along it now, but I do notice the changes.

It's raining even here, although it feels colder. I've been up and down Main Street too many times to count. It's on a hill and leads toward the water. The stores and shops look the same, some freshly painted. The benches are empty—they were a big hangout when we were growing up—and the corner store is deserted. The donut shop seems busy . . . I don't know when it was built . . . after I left.

Oh well . . . to the nursing home.

I arrive and park off to the side in the small parking lot. When I go in, my dad isn't among those sitting around a large Christmas tree in the corner, nor is he watching television. He is in a chair placed near the bay window by himself, looking out at the small wooded area to the side and back of the home.

It's not so easy to smile seeing your dad like this, but what the hell are you supposed to do?

"How are you, Dad?" I ask as happily as I can.

He just blankly sits there.

A nurse says hello and comes over.

"Are you one of his sons?"

I nod.

"Big family. Would you like to move him closer to the Christmas tree?" she asks.

"Maybe after a while," I say.

"Okay." she says. "If there's anything I can do for you, give me a shout."

As she leaves, I turn to Dad and put my hand on his arm. I want to say something to him that will reach back into the past and bring out something for him to recognize and hold onto. But I don't know what to say. I ask him about his day, Christmases of old . . . anything that pops into my head. He doesn't respond to anything really.

I sit for a while. Eventually I move him closer to the Christmas tree. I want to undo the seatbelt, but Dad looks weak, and sometimes he slouches down so low that he looks as if he will fall out of the chair completely.

"It's a nice tree, Dad," I say. "Do you like it? See the lights and decorations?"

I take his hand to get him to touch it. He doesn't respond. In fact, I think maybe he is happier at the window listening to the wind and rain outside.

I rub his arm and shoulder. "It's okay, Dad, it's okay."

"He's been tired today," says a gentle-speaking woman who sits on the other side of the Christmas tree. "He didn't have a good day."

"Hello," I say to her, and she nods her head and returns to her own thoughts while staring at the Christmas tree.

"Do you want some water, Dad? Beer, maybe?"

It is a useless attempt.

After a while, I sit with him in silence, holding his frail and bony hand, patting the back of it to let him know someone was there.

I don't know . . . I just feel awful . . . so I start singing to him. I sing a Christmas carol he always sang to me when I was a child sitting on his knee in my pyjamas, watching the snowfall before it was time for bed. Dad would rub his stubbly face against mine and lightly sing:

> *Lully, Lullay, Thou little tiny Child,*
> *By by, lully, lullay.*
> *Lully, Lullay, Thou little tiny Child,*
> *By by, lully, lullay.*

> *O sisters too, how may we do . . .*

It is all Dad remembers of the words, and it is all I remember too. I hum it for a while, though, but Dad just blankly stares out at the space in front of him.

I put his hand down and walk over to one of the nursing attendants.

"Could I take my father out for a walk? I'm sure if I bundle him up and keep him dry, he'll be fine."

"Ummm . . . I can't authorize that," she says sadly, "not this late in the day."

I look at her and she looks back at me.

"I could check, but they'll just say no without written authorization from your mother."

I continue to look at her.

"Look," she says, "if you don't ask and you take him out, what can I do? I'll just go help Mrs. Johnson back to her room; that will give you a bit of time. There are blankets there and a plastic cover sheet to keep him dry in the closet at the front. Put him into one of those wheelchairs there the big ones don't fit through the door. He has a hat in the closet too. Buckle him in."

"Thank you," I say.

I grab one of the wheelchairs and unstrap Dad from the large chair he is in. He seems happy to go anywhere. I lift him and ease him into the wheelchair. I take some blankets, a hat out of the closet—I didn't know if it is his—and a thin plastic sheet.

I wrap the plastic sheet around most of the upper part of him and the wheelchair. I put the hat on his head, open the door, turn the chair around, and take him outside into the rain.

It is cold and wet as I start to push him along the sidewalk, and at first the rain seems to hurt him. He grimaces. But slowly he stops making a face, and I push him along the uneven sidewalk and speak pleasantries to him.

"It's raining. Rather cold. Rather nasty, I would say. What about you, Dad, think it's rather nasty, do you? Ah, we will get used to it, it's not so bad out. It's Christmas . . . it should snow . . . cold enough."

I push him along and think, What the hell, maybe he will recognize the church he attended for most of his life. When we arrive there is an evening mass going on. I pull him up the stairs and get him inside, at the back of the church. Maybe he will enjoy the choir, he used to love music. But he doesn't respond to any of it. He just has the same blank expression on his face.

After a while, I take him back outside. It has stopped raining, although it is getting quite cold.

Somewhere along our walk back toward the nursing home, I decide to make a short excursion to the house we lived in.

I turn onto a short street and push the wheelchair along a lane toward the back yard. It is dark and muddy. He almost slips out of the wheelchair, and I'm getting mud all over him. Oh well, clean him up later, I say to myself. At the back entrance to the yard, I push him across the wet lawn toward a cluster of birch trees that I remember Dad planting long ago. He planted them for Mom because they were her favourite. I park his wheelchair there, in the center of the yard.

I look at the yard. It seems so different, yet so full of memories.

Despite the cold, I keep him there for a while. At some point when I'm standing there, I notice Dad trying to lean forward. I reach down to steady him. He tries to get up. I put my arm around his waist, unbuckle him, and help him stand slightly. With tears in his eyes, Dad looks out at what was once his own back yard. He looks at the trees, the cedar hedges, and the plot of dirt that was his garden. Then he slowly looks up at the back of his house.

I stand there holding him up as he looks at his yard and home. Then large white flakes of snow start to whirl in the air around us. Dad holds up his hand to catch some. As the snowflakes land on the palm of his hand and melt, he seems to smile and continues looking around the yard.

"Merry Christmas, Dad," I say.

I look at him and try to hug him. It is an awkward attempt. For a moment I think he tries to hug back, but I'm not sure.

Then, as he anxiously looks out at the yard, he starts to hum. He hums the Christmas carol I sang and hummed to him earlier . . . the one he often sang to me when I was a child in pyjamas sitting on his knee, looking out the window at the snow falling. As I hold him up and steady him, he continues to look around and keeps humming, so I sing to him the song he had so often sung to me . . .

> *Lully, Lullay, Thou little tiny Child,*
> *By by, lully, lullay.*
> *Lully, Lullay, Thou little tiny Child,*
> *By by, lully, lullay.*
>
> *O sisters too, how may we do . . .*
> *By by, lully, lullay . . .*

The Christmas Raven

The sun had not yet risen above the horizon.

Tom shut off his alarm as he started to wake up. He rubbed his eyes and lips. He turned his head in one direction and then the other. His arms and legs ached first thing in the morning. Slowly, he bent his knees and wrapped his arms around them, then twisted his torso from side to side to rid himself of his stiffness. He closed his eyes and massaged his misshapen forehead and skull. He had never gotten used to the bumpy feel of his head; it was as if he were touching something not attached to him. His large, uneven forehead felt particularly uneven this morning. His coarse, matted hair stuck out in all directions. He rubbed his eyes again to clear his thoughts and sat up. He squirmed backward, stuffing a pillow behind his back and pulling up the covers and comforter to keep himself warm. He leaned his head against the headboard and took long, deep breaths. In his bed, looking out his window in the quiet stillness of the early morning, he thought, dreamt, hoped, and sometimes fell in and out of sleep. He shook his head to wake up and looked out the partially frosted window in hopes of seeing the sunrise.

Between the trees at the end of the driveway he could see the sky getting lighter. This morning, like most mornings, there were ravens on top of the trees. They too seemed to be awaiting the dawn.

Slowly, the sun peeked over the trees, and its first rays of light seemed to glance off the ravens to light the wall behind him. He raised his hand as if to clasp the rays of sunlight.

Today will be a better day, he thought.

He sat there for a while until the ravens awkwardly flew off. He did not want to go to school today, but he didn't want to stay home and face a barrage of questions. So he moved his body sideways, and with a deep moan, he swung his legs around until he was sitting at the side of the bed. It was cold. He quickly got up and made his way to the washroom, where he showered without wetting his hair and then dressed. Downstairs, he drank a glass of juice, put on his winter coat, opened the side door, and stepped out into the cold. The sky was clear, and there was only a slight wind. As he limped down the driveway, his legs loosened up.

Yesterday had been a bad day at school; he had almost gotten into three separate fights. He did not know exactly when he had reached his toleration point, but he couldn't take being pushed around and made fun of any longer.

A group of twelfth graders had approached Tom yesterday.

"Nice gloves," one boy said to him.

"Let's see your nice gloves," added someone else.

One of them tripped Tom while another grabbed his gloves, throwing each in opposite directions of the hall. He screamed at them and later at anyone who neared him.

He was tired of it all, he thought. He would just try to avoid everyone today. Somehow, he would try to disappear into that oblivion he knew so well as a child, that inner silence where he was alone.

He took out his Walkman, put on his earphones, turned on the music, and flipped the hood of his coat over his head. He walked a little faster along the county road on that brisk December morning, the day of Christmas Eve.

"Christmas . . ." he said, as if to explain the gloom he felt.

* * * * *

Lawrence ran.

He was tall, long-legged, and a fast runner. But he could not run fast enough. Through snow, through long grass, through underbrush, a dog stalked him until he stopped running, until he held his breath and did not move. With cold, alien, lifeless eyes of grey, the dog held him there with the force of its stare. Lawrence tried to achieve perfection in being still. Somehow he knew that if he were still, the dog would not bite him. But it was poised, waiting to attack. Thus, he tried to lay perfectly still while he slept.

He moved his head slowly as he awoke, then startled himself with thoughts of the time. He quickly looked at the clock; it was eleven. That was late for him on a school night, even if tomorrow was only a half-day because it was Christmas Eve.

They had both fallen asleep.

He looked at her as she slept beside him, her head on his arm, he in her bed. Without moving, he shook his head at himself. "Why did I do this?" a sleepy voice inside asked. He could feel himself shrug. It was a confusing thing, for he always irresistibly wanted this but inevitably felt bad.

How did he end up with her when he had decided he was in love with someone else? It was as if the day he decided he loved Eileen, everyone he had ever liked was suddenly interested in him. But why couldn't he just walk away, refuse . . . not want to?

He took a long, deep breath.

"I have to stop," he thought. "There is something wrong here."

By sixteen years of age, Lawrence was tall and handsome. His complexion was clear, except for the developing lines of concern around his mouth and eyes. Everyone told him he was good looking, especially adults. He had been told many times that each step he took, each motion of his hand was a movement of precision, charm, and grace.

He shook his head at himself once more, then glanced over at the clock again. He had to get going.

"Why do I do this?" he asked himself.

He turned to get up, but she put her arm around him.

Lawrence looked down at her. Her skin looked soft and he noticed that she slept with her lips protruding in a pout. Sometimes she stood like that when she was at her desk and about to begin class. He looked at her large breasts. Everyone noticed her breasts, he thought.

He took a couple of deep breaths.

"I've got to go," he said as he pulled his arm out from underneath her head.

She wrapped her arms around him and gently pulled him on top of her.

"Not yet," she said. "In a few minutes."

He tried to smile, then kissed her lips and neck.

*****

Aidan rolled over and got out of bed when he heard the side door close downstairs. He grabbed his bathrobe, stood at the window in the hallway, and picked up a small, carved stone from the windowsill. It was an odd piece of stone, shaped by nature and carved slightly to look like a leaf attached to a twig. Aidan watched Tom in silhouette walk down the sunlit, tree-lined driveway toward the county road to begin his hour-long walk to school.

Aidan used to wake up and prepare breakfast for them, but Tom avoided contact first thing. Now Aidan got out of bed when he heard the side door being closed. For the first few weeks of school, Tom had taken the bus, but that had stopped. Aidan wasn't sure what had happened on the bus, but one morning Tom decided he would walk. He had been getting up early ever since.

He watched Tom limp down the long driveway of the farmhouse. It took Tom a while to get his body working for him, and it made Aidan feel sorry for him. He shook his head at that thought and tried to smile. He was proud of Tom, but his smile had a sadness to it. He was happy that Tom was a part of his life.

He was in his late sixties and raising a young boy. There was joy in that, even if Tom was often sad and without friends. As Tom disappeared beyond the driveway, Aidan gently placed the carved stone back on the windowsill and returned to his room.

Aidan was a tall, thin man with white hair, which he kept cut short. His body was thin and rigid, as if a strong wind had shaped his bones, turned his hair white, weathered his face with liver spots, and brought a permanent stark focus to his darting blue eyes. He yawned and stopped at the top of the stairs, wondering what had happened to Tom yesterday. Tom had said nothing, but Aidan knew something was bothering him; it showed in his walk this morning.

How many times had he watched Tom's silhouette? It was as if he were forever walking from darkness toward light. His first image of Tom was a silhouette against the horizon along the stone fence that separated his property from that of his nearest neighbor. Aidan never knew his new neighbors, except for the fact that they were from town and had two boys. One was killed in a car accident along the concession road two weeks after they moved in. The child was supposed to have been quite a talented ballplayer and good at school. The other apparently had been born with some condition. Aidan remembered that the local papers made quite a fuss over it, but he did not remember why.

Shortly after the car accident, both parents died in a fire that burned the run-down farmhouse to the ground. The youngest was placed in a foster home. He ran away. He was placed in an institution and ran away from there too. Four and a half years ago, the police approached Aidan in the late afternoon to see if he had seen the boy, thinking he had returned to the farm. Aidan told them he had not. But that evening out of his kitchen window as he made dinner, he saw a boy sitting on top of the stone fence that separated his property from that of his neighbor's. The child seemed to be watching the sun set.

Seeing that child alone out there struck him as if someone had pounded his chest with a fist. He had to sit down for a moment. Then a bizarre thought occurred to him. He would adopt this child. "No, I don't need a child to worry over," he had said to himself. Then he stood up to look out the window again.

Aidan smiled and shook his head as he remembered that night. He had thought himself a man who did not want children, who had no time or intention of ever raising a child.

"Why was I so stubborn then?" he asked himself.

"Your stubbornness will make you miserable," she had said to him many times.

And she was right, he thought. That was why he started fighting his stubbornness the day Tom entered his house. Tom to him was the irony of ironies.

Aidan had lost the only woman he ever truly loved because she wanted children almost right away. He was twenty-three then. He had told her, "You'll be miserable without children; I'll be miserable without you; but I'll make us both miserable having children I don't want."

"You are a stubborn man," she had said.

After many tears, they went their separate ways. He heard that after a couple of years she married and started a family. He became even more miserable but never dreamed he would not fall in love again. It was many years before the ache in his heart subsided at all. Maybe it never entirely left him until that evening when he saw the boy alone on the stone fence. Something within him shifted. When he turned away from the window, he cooked dinner for himself and made a second plate. When he got out to the stone fence, there was no one there. But he left the plate of food and some water for the boy. He did this each evening.

He could not remember how long that went on for, but it seemed like weeks. Then one evening, the young boy left him a carved stone that looked like a leaf attached to a twig. That night, Aidan decided to talk to the boy, but the boy did not come out from hiding.

"Young man," he said aloud, hoping the boy would hear, "tomorrow you will come to my place for dinner; you don't have to stay. It'll be just you and me. If you decide to stay, you can . . . if you want to leave, you can. Come when you wish to. Just knock on the door . . ."

He put a plate of food down on the usual rock and left. The next afternoon he returned to the stone fence to find the plate untouched.

"My oh my," he said to himself.

Yet that night the boy stood outside Aidan's kitchen window, looking as if he had tried to wash. Aidan opened the door and invited him in. The boy stepped inside the door. He was the ugliest child Aidan had ever seen. He had a large, uneven head that seemed made from a few broken pieces of porcelain glued back together. One ear was lower than the other; his eyes were dark and deeply set. He had no lips except a line of dirt that outlined his mouth. Aidan swallowed hard and asked the child to come in and pointed to a seat at the dining room table. He asked him his name and many other things, but the child did not answer. They ate in silence. When they were finished, Aidan showed him a room he could sleep in "if you want to. If not tonight, then on other nights, when it gets cold," he had said. The boy left but later returned with a tattered suitcase. He had been with Aidan since.

"What's your name?" asked Aidan, opening the door when the boy returned with his suitcase.

"TOM . . . TOM MCINTYRE."

He spoke with a deep voice that boomed outward, as if he spoke directly from his chest. It was a loud burst of sound: coarse, deep, and animal-like. Yet he spoke coherently and seemed to understand everything Aidan said to him.

That first weekend, Aidan bought him some clothes and took him to a junior league baseball game in town.

"I WANT TO BE A BASEBALL PLAYER," he announced afterward.

Aidan nodded his head.

"Well, you'll have to work hard," said Aidan.

"I WILL," stated Tom.

Shortly after that, Aidan enrolled Tom in school. He worked with Tom to help him learn what he had to know for grade seven. Tom could read and write, and Aidan found him to be intelligent, though stubborn.

"I DON'T CARE ABOUT SCHOOL. I WANT TO BE A BASE-BALL PLAYER."

"Let's get you in school first, then we'll get you into a baseball league if we can," Aidan told him.

"LAST TIME THEY SENT ME TO RETARD SCHOOL."

"Well, not this time," said Aidan.

The day Tom came home from his first day in grade seven, Aidan bought him a baseball and glove.

Aidan never told Tom how much effort it had taken to get him a chance to try out for the Junior Bantam baseball team. Junior Bantam was a selected inter-county and inter-district team for twelve- to fourteen-year-olds. Aidan remembered how much Tom ran every day, played catch, and practiced. Aidan bought him rubber balls that he could throw against the brick wall of the side of the farmhouse. He threw those rubber balls until they were worn-out and shredded, as if a dog had chewed them.

Aidan remembered how badly Tom limped the first day of practice and how nervous he was. But he made the team and seemed estatic about it, even if he spent most of his time on the bench. He wore his uniform everywhere, and for the first few weeks, he even slept with it on. The coach kept him on the team because Tom tried so hard. As Aidan found out later, Tom never played more than one inning. He had played left field during one game, halfway through the season. Two balls got by him. One, a high fly ball that would have been the final out, cost them the game. Tom had returned home hurt badly. His face was bloody and torn. Aidan helped clean his cuts and bandage them. Then later that evening, from the dining room window, he sadly watched as Tom sat on the grass where so many times he had thrown the rubber balls against the wall, reacting over and over again, as if an invisible marksman had shot him in the shoulder, while he looked high into the sky with his glove hand extended upward.

* * * * *

Many times Tom saw that high fly ball hang in the breeze. He had run rather awkwardly to get under it but was there in time, waiting as the ball came down. It smacked against his collarbone and bounced away from him as he fell to the ground. The game was over. He remained on the ground as the coach and others rushed toward him. He just shook his head when they asked him to get up, and he stayed on the ground with his face buried in his glove. He didn't cry, he didn't speak, he didn't move.

Eventually, when they left him alone and everyone was gone, he turned over. It was all he could do to not cry. He lay there on the grass, grinding his teeth together, looking up into the peaceful blue sky, not wanting to move, not wanting to play baseball anymore.

Since seeing his brother play baseball, he had dreamt about wanting to be a baseball player. To have grace, effortlessly making great catches . . . that was what he wanted to do. It was a promise to himself. Alone, he would try to exercise each day so that he might one day play well. His young mind would whirl with dreams of running with speed, smoothly jumping up, up, up before the fence, and with perfect precision, plucking the ball out of the air as it soared to clear the fence.

He wasn't sure how long he lay in the field. When he got up, he limped to the pitching mound. He stood there looking around at the field, at the backstop, at the bleachers . . . Then he looked beyond the parking lot toward the horizon and the blue sky. He watched a raven flying over the tops of the trees as if it were searching for another day.

He took off his baseball cap and tucked it inside his glove. He placed them down on the ground. Then he stood and stared at home plate. To be graceful, he thought, to move as if motion were the most natural thing in the world . . .

For a moment he looked back at left field. Then he took a deep breath, turned, and ran as fast and as gracefully as he had ever run. With his most determined show of coordination and dexterity, he approached home plate. His legs and arms pumped smoothly with speed and power as he passed over it. For a moment he felt as if he might run right through the chain-link fence. That thought stayed with him as his arms and legs reached the fence, only slightly hindered. The thought vanished when he felt the aluminum pierce his face and nose. His forward movement stopped. He felt throbs of sharp pain as the chain-link metal met the bone of his skull.

"Figures," a voice from inside of him said.

He was stuck to the fence and did not move. Then, suddenly, he felt an overwhelming thrust of pain from everywhere as his skin and flesh grew warm and would not hold his weight. He collapsed to the ground, semi-conscious. His entire body was numb. He closed his eyes, and his mind's vision seemed to burst into countless particles of white and orange light that collected across his field of sight. He tried to look toward the light, to see into it. Out of those particles of light an angel spoke to him. Her face was luminous and warm. There was care and gentleness in her voice as she reached out to touch his arm. She seemed to float in the air above him, wearing a soft white dress that swept over the grass as she moved. He tried to reach out and touch her so that he might know if she was real, but he did not seem able to.

He heard the angel whisper to him, "You'll be okay."

He tried to see her, but it was as if a ray of light had spoken to him, had touched and kissed his hand.

He tried to reach out to touch her again, but she seemed to fly straight upward. This made everything spin around him. Then he felt himself float upward, as if they were together on a cloud, her saying things to him he did not understand, him smiling, knowing he now had a friend.

* * * * *

Eileen stood in front of the mirror. She stood with a soft lace shawl across her shoulders as she brushed her wet hair back from her face. She was alone in her room, posing in front of the mirror. She had had a bath and was hoping Lawrence would call while she was still warm and not wearing clothes.

She looked at her breasts. They were filling out, but they were not as large as she would have liked them to be. She wanted breasts like Ms. Cavenleigh, her English teacher, although she never told anyone that. She had done exercises in her room and tried a special diet to make them larger, but nothing worked. She thought her life would be better if she had larger breasts. She was sure she was the only one in class who still had not had sex and blamed it on that fact. Being a good girl was an awkwardness that wouldn't go away. When she first dated Lawrence, she thought this would end on their first date. But many dates later, they seemed no further along. She had been patient with Lawrence to initiate things, but it wasn't happening.

She never expected to have this problem. Her parents had warned her over and over about boys for all her years growing up, but despite being told she was attractive, no boys had tried anything with her. So far, Lawrence had been a perfect gentleman, which was good, but it also meant he wouldn't put a hand on her. She had tried to convey her willingness, but he did not seem to notice. That would change, she thought. On Christmas Eve her parents were going out, and she would tie him to her bed if she had to. She had felt somewhat encouraged today when Lawrence walked her home after school and kissed her as if he were thinking about doing it right there. Their lips and bodies worked together, and she felt herself go limp.

"Things are going to change," she had said to herself with excitement.

She loved the feel of his lips and imagined them kissing her everywhere. She had tried to hold him longer, pressing herself against him, but he stopped as if sensing her willingness.

She looked at her bed and the phone on the side table. She hoped he would call.

She walked over to the large sliding doors of her bedroom, which led out to the large sun deck at the back of the house. She looked out the window toward the baseball park as she continued to brush her hair. The park was dark, except for the streetlights on either side. She thought about how many times she had played baseball in the park with the boys and how many times she had watched them. She had always been a bit of a tomboy. Their house was just on the other side of Wilfred Creek, beyond right field. She had often walked over to the hill on the other side of the creek, beyond the first baseline, and watched the boys. Even years ago she remembered liking Lawrence and going to the games to watch him play. She knew nothing about him except that he played third base and was good looking.

One day she wore a dress. She sat in the field on the warm grass, hoping that somehow he would just notice her and come over. That's what boys were supposed to do, her mom had said. That same game, she remembered, poor Tom had tried to catch a fly ball. When she saw the ball hit him, she turned the other way, afraid to look. When she looked back toward him, he was lying on the ground, motionless. He did not get up. Others went out to check on him, but he just lay there. Then after a time, everyone left him alone, the small set of bleachers emptied, and she left too. When she got home and went to her room to change, out of her window, looking in the distance, she noticed Tom still on the ground.

The thought occurred to her that maybe he was dead. She stood there for a moment, then quickly ran downstairs, out the door, and back to the baseball park. When she crossed the bridge over the creek and reached the hill that extended off to the side of the first baseline, she saw him standing on the pitcher's mound. She watched him stand there. He put his cap into his baseball glove and put his glove on the ground. He glanced behind him, then toward home plate. Then she watched him run as fast as he could for home plate, except he did not stop. This confused her—then he ran into the chain-link fence.

She screamed and ran toward him.

By the time she reached him, he was lying on the ground.

She ran up to him to see what she could do. He was moaning; there was blood everywhere.

"You'll be okay," she cried.

She leaned over him, and he raised his hand to her; she grabbed his hand, held it for a moment, and brought it to her lips before placing it on his chest. She turned and ran as fast as she could.

"Dad," she screamed as she neared the house. "Dad, a boy's been hurt."

Her father came up the stairs, and together they ran to the park. When they got there, Tom was gone.

"He was right here," she said.

"I guess he is okay," said her father.

As she stood in front of the sliding doors, brushing her hair, she recalled vividly how bloody his face had been. She still felt sorry for him to this day. He had such an ugly face . . . and so many of the girls at school were afraid of him . . . some teased him . . . and the boys were cruel. She looked out beyond the creek, the hill, and the pitching mound to the spot in the chain-link fence that for a long time held the impression of Tom's oddly shaped head. She had not checked the spot for a couple of years now, but she had often showed it to others at the time.

She started to shiver as she stood in front of the sliding glass doors.

"Please call," she whispered, thinking of Lawrence.

She stopped brushing her hair and turned to her closet to get some clothes on.

* * * * *

Aidan got dressed, poured himself some coffee, and went out to the shed to see how Tom's work had progressed.

Thirty years ago, Aidan turned what as at one time a horse barn into a work shed. He was a glassmaker, and he thought Tom talented. He had recently tried to get a journalist from the local paper to look at Tom's work, but the journalist was only interested if it included getting an update on Tom's health. Aidan just shook his head.

Last year, Tom made a dish for a girl at school. It had been a good piece, only Tom didn't have the courage to give it to her. Again this year, Aidan knew he was making a piece for this girl . . . It was shaping up to be his best piece yet. Every day since Tom started the project, Aidan made a point of checking it. This year he would make sure Tom gave it to her.

Aidan thought Tom too quiet at times. He often brooded, as if he thought others stood around thinking about how ugly he was. Aidan assured him they didn't. But Tom was suspicious of people. So much so that even when Aidan wanted to take him to the doctor to get the cuts on his face dressed or stitched if necessary, Tom refused.

"THEY'LL WANT TO SHAVE MY HEAD AND TAKE A PICTURE. I'M NOT A FREAK. I'M FINE. I'M ALWAYS FINE," Tom had said.

So Aidan dressed his cuts as he listened to Tom tell him how he had been running for a fly ball—the fastest he had ever run—and ran into the left field fence.

He quit the team after that. Aidan wanted him to continue playing, but Tom announced his decision in the same manner he announced anything he decided.

"IT WASN'T MEANT TO BE," he said.

"Who told you that?" asked Aidan.

"NO ONE TOLD ME. I CAN SEE IT NOW."

"We should take you to see a doctor."

"I'M FINE. I'M ALWAYS FINE," he said to Aidan.

He knew that although Tom was not badly injured, he wasn't fine. After dressing Tom's cuts, Aidan helped him outside to sit on the grass and called the coach to ask if anything had happened to cause Tom to not want to play anymore.

"He missed a fly ball," said the coach. "The ball hit him pretty hard. We thought he was hurt, but he was more embarrassed than anything. And he missed a grounder before that. He was okay, just upset that he had missed the balls."

"He didn't run into the left field fence?" asked Aidan.

"A fence? No, he was nowhere near a fence. He missed a pop-up in shallow left field, and the ball hit him pretty good. Nothing broken or anything like that, though."

After that Tom no longer asked Aidan to play catch with him. He no longer threw the ball against the side of the house, no longer ran in the field, chasing after a ball he had thrown into the air.

Aidan did not like this silence Tom lived in. He did not like not knowing what had happened on the bus to school. He did not like not knowing what had happened that day he ran into the fence. He did not like the lies. He did not like the omissions. Nor did he like the silent, moody evenings after a difficult day at school.

It was shortly after quitting baseball that Tom stood at the window of the shed behind the house staring in, watching Aidan work. Aidan noticed him at the window, thinking that perhaps something had happened. He had quickly resigned himself to letting Tom tell him in his own good time when things troubled him. Aidan tried not to look toward him. He saw Tom but continued rolling a piece of glass, getting it ready to put back into the furnace. After a while, Tom opened the door and stepped inside the shed and waited for Aidan to step away from the furnace.

"I NEED TO LEARN A TRADE," Tom said when Aidan looked at him. "I WANT TO WORK FOR YOU."

Aidan stopped and looked at Tom.

"So baseball is out, and now I'm a tradesman, and you want to be one too."

"YES."

"It may shock you, but I don't consider this a trade, young man."

"WHAT IS IT?"

"I don't know. A life, maybe." He looked around at his shop. "So now suddenly this is the kind of life you want?"

"YES."

"What for? So you can quit it like baseball when things don't work out?"

"NO, BASEBALL IS DIFFERENT. I'M NOT GOOD AT IT.

THIS I WILL WORK HARD AT. I PROMISE YOU THAT."

"Quitters don't get far," said Aidan.

"I WON'T BE A QUITTER. YOU WON'T BE DISAPPOINT-ED. YOU WILL SEE."

"It's you I'm worried about," said Aidan.

"I'M FINE. I'M ALWAYS FINE."

Aidan looked at him.

"You are not always fine, Tom. No one is."

Tom frowned and turned as if he were about to leave.

"Well, when would you like to start?" asked Aidan.

"RIGHT NOW," said Tom.

Aidan took a deep breath and slowly looked around at the horse barn he had converted into his work shed. He looked out the windows at the large elms and maples that surrounded it. Then he looked at the furnace, his workstations, and at Tom.

Did Tom have any idea how much he had put into this? Any idea how much of his life was in this shop? An inkling of what his work meant to him? How hard he had worked to at first get by, then get good at it? Probably not, thought Aidan, but maybe it would be good to have someone to work with.

What could he get Tom to work on, he wondered. He looked at the main floor area, which was one large room with a furnace built into one side of the shed. The metal furnace was set in large masonry stone and had a sliding door across it. Several long pieces of iron pipe dangled on racks on either side of the door. Two workstations had benches with metal pipe handles for rolling the blowing rods. A flat piece of metal used for shaping hot glass sat on an old sewing machine cabinet in front of one of the stations. Over the years, he had collected anything he could use in his workshop. He had turned old rain barrels into wooden moulds. He had a lot of them lining the wall opposite the furnace; some steamed and hissed as they cooled. Near the far end of the shed, Aidan had placed a large blue machine that had once been used for making milkshakes. He had bought it and converted it into a machine to file his glassware.

He looked at Tom.

"What actually happened to your face?"

Tom looked at him.

"I WAS BORN THIS WAY."

"No, no, the cuts on your face, from baseball," said Aidan.

"I RAN INTO A FENCE."

"You missed a pop-up."

Tom seemed surprised by this.

"YES. BUT THEN I RAN INTO THE FENCE."

"When?"

"AFTER THE GAME."

"On purpose?"

"YES."

"Why did you do that?"

Tom hesitated.

"I RAN INTO THE FENCE 'CAUSE I WAS MAD."

"Why were you so mad?"

"'CAUSE I'M NO GOOD AT BASEBALL."

"Well, we don't get mad like that around here. At least there are no fences around here to run into. We talk when we get mad, which will happen when you make glass. Is that clear?"

Tom nodded.

"Good. Then you can start. Hang up your jacket."

Aidan slowly rubbed his chin. "Well, where should we begin? What do you want to learn?"

"EVERYTHING," said Tom.

"Everything. Well, let's start with something simple. There, see the sand I've put in those two buckets? We'll start by making glass like they did thousands of years ago. We'll make a mould of various leaf shapes. So out you go to collect about a dozen large leaves. We'll press them into the wet sand first, and then we will pour molten glass onto it and see what we get. Out you go. Don't be long."

Aidan tried not to look out the window. He wasn't sure if Tom would like being told what to do. But a short while later, Tom came in with the leaves. He showed Tom how to press them into the sand to create a pattern and how to pour molten glass onto it.

When they had finished with the plates, Aidan pointed to several moulds in the corner and told Tom to get them.

"You can help me with these wooden moulds to make glass pitchers. This piece of flat metal is a marver; that is a blowing tube, as are all those ones hanging on the rack," he said, pointing to them. "This is a punty," he said, holding out a tool that looked like a small crowbar, "and these are tweezers. Both are useful in shaping molten glass." He held out the large, heavy tweezers for Tom to hold, but Tom did not take them.

Aidan looked down at him. Tom already looked bored.

Aidan stood in frustrated silence, not sure of what to do.

He shrugged.

"Okay, forget all this," he said and grabbed Tom roughly by the arm and led him to the furnace.

"Here, take hold of one of these," he said and forcefully handed Tom a long, hollow bar and then opened the door of the hot furnace. "Stick it into the middle there where the canister of molten glass is. No, no, not there. Right in the middle," he said as he guided Tom's iron bar to the pot. "There, you have it."

Tom watched as the glowing, sticky, thick molten glass stuck to the metal tube he was holding.

"Now . . ." Aidan grabbed another metal tube, ". . . carefully take it out." He pushed the second tube against the first so that the glass stuck to both. "Carefully . . . slowly . . . place it over here, and I'll cut some off. It's a bit too big to start with," he said as he took some oversized scissors and cut some of the molten glass so that it dropped onto the pipe he was holding. He returned it to the furnace. "There now. Sit here and roll the pipe along these arm bars, just back and forth like this." As he helped Tom roll the pipe back and forth, the glass developed an elongated, round shape.

Tom's eyes widened. He stared at the molten glass as if it mesmerized him. Then he raised his head and smiled at Aidan.

"Never mind, never mind. Pay attention, keep your focus. Let's go . . ."

He watched Tom carefully roll the iron bar back and forth with the molten glass stuck on the end of it. His eyes were riveted to it as if it might come to life at any moment before him and he did not want to miss it.

"It's your bubble," said Aidan. "Keep rolling it, and I'll show you how these tools work."

He showed Tom how to swing the rod back and forth to give the glass a smooth shape. He grabbed hold of the tweezers and slowly pressed down on the top of the molten glass and made a vaselike lip on the glass.

Tom could hardly believe his eyes.

"It's like making music. To make good music takes a hell of a long time. I'll tell you that. You have to think to develop your concentration skills. Some of it's just to fill out orders, but other times you can develop your own ideas. This is the most exciting thing of all. Then you will see, you need the thinking and physical skill to know that your hands are doing exactly what your head requests, when it requests it. At any given moment something can and will go wrong. That's good. Mistakes are inevitable and are the best teachers. Mistakes don't lie.

"Stand back," he said sharply.

Tom watched as Aidan moved into the chair and with lightning speed took hold of the pipe. His hands and wrists moved as if choreographed to unheard music. Tom could not believe Aidan could move with such efficiency and grace. His hands moved independent of his white hair and frail arms.

"Now cover the end of the tube with your hands and blow into them. Blow consistently, with a steady firm breath, so that we get some shape to this," he commanded.

Tom took a deep breath and stepped toward Aidan.

"Come on, grab the pipe and hold it like this, downward. It's heavier than you think. Hold it and give it a try."

Tom held it to his small dark lips and blew gently.

"Harder, gradually," said Aidan.

Tom looked at Aidan and then blew harder, but still the molten glass did not react.

"Steady, and harder still," said Aidan.

Tom blew harder and immediately stopped when he saw the molten glass expand outward at the other end.

"It's okay," said Aidan, "we can go a little further than that. Once more . . ."

Tom blew, and the glass expanded like a living, glowing balloon.

Tom looked at Aidan and smiled.

"Never mind, admire it after it's finished. Now start rolling it again, and use this punty to help shape the sides and the bottom. It's yours now; it's your own bubble. Make the most of it."

Aidan watched Tom for a few minutes.

"The art of glassmaking is in going back and doing it over again. You will see. But in each effort, the spirit of the bubble is there, waiting for you to shape it, command it, and make it yours if you have learned your lessons."

Tom continued to roll it along the arm bars of the work chair.

"Slow it down, slow it down," said Aidan, watching him. "Get the feel of when it sags. Not so fast. That's it . . ."

He watched Tom carefully.

"If all goes well, you will learn to speak with your hands. You'll see, the glass listens."

Tom looked at the glow of the red-hot glass. Its deep red light seemed like a pulse of life from the centre of its loose form. He watched it take shape as he rolled the metal bar back and forth. He rolled it slowly, over and over, not daring to take his eyes off the glowing red bubble. It looked like a large light bulb that was attached to the end of the metal tube he held, and it seemed to have a voice that softly hissed at him.

As Aidan looked at Tom, he thought of how there are points in life when one experiences vision. He could see that Tom had found something of himself in this. Aidan always believed there were points in life when all that could be seen was a stretch of road before you that was your own soul. Tom is seeing this road, he thought as he watched Tom look at the glowing red bubble.

I will give you everything I have to offer, my son, thought Aidan. I will give you all that I know . . .

Tom stared at his creation with a mixture of determination and conviction. He rolled it, shaped it, and watched it take form. Aidan pointed to a water bucket for cooling, and Tom carefully submerged the glass for a moment before Aidan showed him where to place it.

Tom gazed around at the shed, the furnace, and then back at his bottle-shaped glass. The now-hardened glass was so smooth, so fluid, so promising. By rolling the iron pipe along the arms of the chair, the glass had developed a general consistency of shape he would never have imagined. Tom shook his head as he looked at what he had made. A spirit had pulsed within the glow of molten glass, and it came to life in his hands. It was a living fluid, smooth, graceful—a vision of something he did not understand.

"Yes," he said to himself.

In certainty, he thought all of life should be like this glowing bubble of glass. He shook his head in affirmation. The thought made him cry.

"What's wrong?" asked Aidan.

"I DON'T KNOW," said Tom. "I THINK I'M HAPPY."

"You have an odd way of showing it," said Aidan.

That was all either of them said. The tears poured down Tom's cheeks like never before, and he started to shake in fits of tears mixed with awkward attempts at smiling.

Tom held his head up as best he could. After a while, he could take deep comforting breaths, only to cry again.

* * * * *

Aidan opened the door. He smiled to himself as he entered his shed. He always entered his workshop with excitement and joy. He was about to make his way to the back of the shed when he noticed Tom's work placed on the stone table at Aidan's workstation. That was where Tom put his finished pieces when he wanted Aidan to see them.

At first Tom made simple glasses, bottles, and plates. Soon he learned to shape, file, and polish glass and made some candleholders and bookends. He then began to experiment. He carved stone, blew glass, and tried to combine them. He often tried to cover the carved stone with molten glass. It seemed impossible. He poured molten glass onto a shaped stone so that the glass would take its shape. It did not work. After many tries, he consulted Aidan, who showed him how to get glass to cover an object. He blew the molten glass into a glowing bubble. He cut out one side of the molten glass and put a stone inside of it. Then he let the molten glass cool and slowly drop onto the stone. It took the stone's shape, but cracked and shattered.

For almost a year now, each night, Tom had been working on one piece. Aidan often came back to the shed late at night to find him there.

"Time for bed," Aidan would command. "You have school tomorrow."

"JUST A COUPLE MORE MINUTES," said Tom.

"I'll give you a couple more minutes all right," said Aidan. "In fact, I'll not let you in here for a week, and you can have all the minutes you want."

"OKAY, I'M GOING . . . NIGHT."

"Good night," said Aidan.

As Tom left the shed each evening, making his way toward the house, Aidan would quickly check Tom's progress, knowing he would not help, yet wanting to more than he could bear. Last night Tom had worked even later than usual.

And there it was, finished . . . It was a bird roughly sculptured in stone, and three-quarters of it was covered with thick, smooth glass. It looked menacing, powerful, and enticing. Its depth seemed to come from out of the stone that made up the core of the bird's body. The bird's glass eyes pierced the air in front of it. Its glass beak was closed, and it was lowering its stone and glass head slightly, as if in thought.

Aidan walked around it slowly.

"My oh my," he said.

Through the glass, Aidan thought he could see that something had been carved into the stone chest of the bird. It was almost unidentifiable, but from two different angles, he could see carved into the stone a young bird's deformed face with its mouth open, screaming.

"My oh my," he repeated.

He stepped back and looked at it again. He stood there for quite some time. He picked it up to hold it, then looked at the bottom. It read: To E—T.M.

Aidan just nodded his head.

* * * * *

It took a while for Tom's legs to loosen up. Each morning he fought with them that he might walk straight. His gait was deliberate, slow, and disjointed. But as he walked, it became less of an effort. He tried each morning to perfect a walk that would hide his limp. His limp belied who he was, he thought, as did his smile. And nothing showed his ugliness more than his smile. He practiced not smiling each morning too, while he walked to school. He developed a smile that was more a squinting of the eyes than a movement of the lips. He had been born this way, and there was nothing he could do about it, he reminded himself. "I'M NOT A FREAK," he repeated aloud to himself regularly. The word freak had a vividness that would not let him know peace. This left him with feelings and desires for simple things: to walk straight, to not be pitied, to have a friend.

As he neared the school, he saw them together at the far entrance. Lawrence stood leaning back against the wall as Eileen stood in front of him. She put her arms around his neck with determination. Tom watched her close her eyes and open her mouth; he lowered his head and limped inside.

How he longed to be kissed with such conviction, he thought. How he longed to have someone look at him and hold him as she held Lawrence. He had seen others look at and hold Lawrence that way, including Ms. Cavenleigh. As he pulled the heavy doors open, he ground his teeth as the image of Eileen and Lawrence together played in his mind over and over again.

Yesterday, between classes, after several boys had taken his gloves, he had yelled at Lawrence because Lawrence and others had teased him. Someone had tripped him again, and he had threatened all of them. His threats had almost gotten him into a fight with a couple of boys. Many had mocked, tripped, and pushed him around at school before. Now he was tired of it and wouldn't take it anymore. He tried to control his anger, but he found himself issuing more threats and feeling more violent.

School had been a hope and a promise for him, especially high school. It was a hope that one day he would be educated and have friends. And he was blessed, he told himself. Eileen was in his English class, and on occasion, when no one was watching, he would steal a casual look in her direction. Never right at her, but just a glance at her side of the room. He wouldn't do anything to embarrass her. And where else would he be able to see her? That was all he ever wanted, he thought, to sit in the same room and on occasion hear her speak, to be delighted by the colors she wore and notice how carefully she wrote in her notebook.

Others would always tease him; he would try to avoid them. When the morning announcements were finished, he made his way to his English class. He walked to the back of the class and sat at his desk, telling himself he would not say a word. As he sat there, Ms Cavenleigh came into the room.

"They would like to see you in the office," she told Tom.

She nodded for him to go as others started to come into the classroom.

Tom got up and went to the office, only to be told a

teacher had reported that he had been yelling in the hallway yesterday. He was told yelling wasn't allowed, and he was given a detention slip. When he returned to class, Ms. Cavenleigh was getting ready to read at the front of the class. She stopped and waved him to his seat.

He walked to his desk at the back of the room.

"Today we are discussing 'The Raven,' by Edgar Allan Poe." She cleared her throat and began.

Once upon a midnight dreary, while I pondered, weak and weary,
Over many a quaint and curious volume of forgotten lore—
While I nodded, nearly napping, suddenly there came a tapping,
As of some one gently rapping, rapping at my chamber door—
"'Tis some visiter," I muttered, "tapping at my chamber door—
        Only this and nothing more."

Ah, distinctly I remember it was in the bleak December;
And each separate dying ember wrought its ghost upon the floor.
Eagerly I wished the morrow;—vainly I had tried to borrow
From my books surcease of sorrow—sorrow for the lost Lenore—
For the rare and radiant maiden whom the angels name Lenore—
        Nameless here for evermore.

And the silken, sad, uncertain rustling of each purple curtain
Thrilled me—filled me with fantastic terrors never felt before;
So that now, to still the beating of my heart, I stood repeating
"'Tis some visiter entreating entrance at my chamber door—
Some late visiter entreating entrance at my chamber door—
        This it is and nothing more."

Presently my soul grew stronger; hesitating then no longer,
"Sir," said I, "or Madam, truly your forgiveness I implore;
But the fact is I was napping, and so gently you came rapping,
And so faintly you came tapping, tapping at my chamber door,
That I scarce was sure I heard you"—here I opened wide the door;—
        Darkness there and nothing more.

Deep into that darkness peering, long I stood there wondering, fearing,
Doubting, dreaming dreams no mortal ever dared to dream before;
But the silence was unbroken, and the darkness gave no token,
And the only word there spoken was the whispered word, "Lenore!"
This I whispered, and an echo murmured back the word, "Lenore!"
*   Merely this and nothing more.*

Then into the chamber turning, all my soul within me burning,
Soon I heard again a tapping somewhat louder than before.
"Surely," said I, "surely that is something at my window lattice;
Let me see, then, what thereat is, and this mystery explore—
Let my heart be still a moment and this mystery explore;—
*   'Tis the wind and nothing more!"*

Open here I flung the shutter, when, with many a flirt and flutter,
In there stepped a stately Raven of the saintly days of yore;
Not the least obeisance made he; not an instant stopped or stayed he;
But, with mien of lord or lady, perched above my chamber door—
Perched upon a bust of Pallas just above my chamber door—
*   Perched, and sat, and nothing more.*

Then this ebony bird beguiling my sad fancy into smiling,
By the grave and stern decorum of the countenance it wore,
"Though thy crest be shorn and shaven, thou," I said, "art sure no
*   craven,*
Ghastly grim and ancient Raven wandering from the Nightly shore—
Tell me what thy lordly name is on the Night's Plutonian shore!"
*   Quoth the Raven "Nevermore."*

Much I marvelled this ungainly fowl to hear discourse so plainly,
Though its answer little meaning—little relevancy bore;
For we cannot help agreeing that no sublunary being
Ever yet was blessed with seeing bird above his chamber door—
Bird or beast upon the sculptured bust above his chamber door,
*   With such a name as "Nevermore."*

But the Raven, sitting lonely on the placid bust, spoke only
That one word, as if his soul in that one word he did outpour.
Nothing farther then he uttered—not a feather then he fluttered—
Till I scarcely more than muttered "Other friends have flown before—
On the morrow he will leave me, as my Hopes have flown before."
       Quoth the Raven "Nevermore."

Wondering at the stillness broken by reply so aptly spoken,
"Doubtless," said I, "what it utters is its only stock and store
Caught from some unhappy master whom unmerciful Disaster
Followed fast and followed faster so, when Hope he would adjure
Stern Despair returned, instead of the sweet Hope he dared adjure—
       That sad answer, "Nevermore!"

But the Raven still beguiling all my sad soul into smiling,
Straight I wheeled a cushioned seat in front of bird, and bust and door;
Then, upon the velvet sinking, I betook myself to linking
Fancy unto fancy, thinking what this ominous bird of yore—
What this grim, ungainly, ghastly, gaunt, and ominous bird of yore
       Meant in croaking "Nevermore."

This I sat engaged in guessing, but no syllable expressing
To the fowl whose fiery eyes now burned into my bosom's core;
This and more I sat divining, with my head at ease reclining
On the cushion's velvet lining that the lamp-light gloated o'er,
But whose velvet-violet lining with the lamp-light gloating o'er,
       She shall press, ah, nevermore!

Then, methought, the air grew denser, perfumed from an unseen censer
Swung by angels whose faint foot-falls tinkled on the tufted floor.
"Wretch," I cried, "thy God hath lent thee—by these angels he hath
    sent thee
Respite—respite and nepenthe from thy memories of Lenore;
Let me quaff this kind nepenthe and forget this lost Lenore!"
       Quoth the Raven "Nevermore."

"Prophet!" said I, "thing of evil!—prophet still, if bird or devil!—
Whether Tempter sent, or whether tempest tossed thee here ashore,
Desolate yet all undaunted, on this desert land enchanted—
On this home by Horror haunted—tell me truly, I implore—
Is there—is there blame in Gilead?—tell me—tell me, I implore!"
      Quoth the Raven "Nevermore."

"Prophet!" said I, "thing of evil!—prophet still, if bird or devil!
By that Heaven that bends above us—by that God we both adore—
Tell this soul with sorrow laden if, within the distant Aidenn,
It shall clasp a sainted maiden whom the angels name Lenore—
Clasp a rare and radiant maiden whom the angels name Lenore."
      Quoth the Raven "Nevermore."

"Be that word our sign of parting, bird or fiend!" I shrieked,
    upstarting—
"Get thee back into the tempest and the Night's Plutonian shore!
Leave no black plume as a token of that lie thy soul hath spoken!
Leave my loneliness unbroken!—quit the bust above my door!
Take thy beak from out my heart, and take thy form from off my door!"
      Quoth the Raven "Nevermore."

And the Raven, never flitting, still is sitting, still is sitting
On the pallid bust of Pallas just above my chamber door;
And his eyes have all the seeming of a demon that is dreaming,
And the lamp-light o'er him streaming throws his shadow on the floor;
And my soul from out that shadow that lies floating on the floor
      Shall be lifted—nevermore!

Ms. Cavenleigh gave the class a couple of minutes as she returned to sit behind her desk. She looked around the classroom at her students to see if anyone cared to start the discussion.

"Who can tell me," she asked, "why the Raven says 'Nevermore'?"

Tom closed his eyes for a moment and took a deep breath. There was silence. No one said anything. He watched Ms. Cavenleigh look from row to row.

"Now think, why 'Nevermore'?" she asked. "Anyone? Any thoughts?"

She looked out at her students. Her idea to spend one class every two weeks in appreciation of poetry that the students chose had been popular in the beginning of the year, but by the end of term everyone grew bored with it, and it had become progressively more difficult to start a class discussion. She had hoped the discussion would go quickly because she wanted to read a poem with a Christmas theme.

Tom studiously avoided her gaze, and he noticed others doing the same.

"Well, no thoughts in anyone's head . . . ?" she said, coming out from behind her desk as if to let them know they couldn't hide. "Come on, it's not that difficult. Are we just a little premature in our Christmas holiday state of mind? Come on, a bit more of an effort. Eileen? What do you think?"

Eileen gave an exaggerated look of ignorance and gently shrugged her shoulders.

"Who chose this poem?" Ms. Cavenleigh asked.

No one answered.

"Oh, I suppose no one did?"

She waited.

She was not going to stand there in silence much longer, she thought. "Well, come on. Anyone? Did anyone like the poem?"

No one said anything.

"Nothing in our heads today?" she asked.

No one answered.

"Come on, people, wake up. How many of you read this poem before class?"

No one looked at her.

"Did no one read it?"

"I DID," said Tom reluctantly.

Everyone turned around to look at Tom.

"Nice voice," Tom heard someone say.

Tom tried to clear his throat.

"All right now, all right," said Ms. Cavenleigh, "that's enough."

She looked at Tom with pity. "Life has not been so kind to you, has it?" she had said to him at the beginning of the term when he was sitting alone in her class.

"I don't need your pity," he had snapped.

It was only later that Tom realized she was probably trying to be kind.

Everyone in town and at school knew about him from the newspapers. He had seen newspaper clippings in an old shoebox in the attic when he was younger.

"Wrongful Life," one headline stated. "I Should Never Have Been Born," said another with a picture of him. It was an ugly sight, and he could not stand to look at the photograph. The newspaper articles reported that his mother had contracted chicken pox when she was in her twelfth week of pregnancy. Her doctor informed her that there was a small risk to her fetus of developing a limb and skin disorder called congenital varicella syndrome. She was assured that the risks were small, and so they did not recommend aborting the fetus. Nevertheless, the child was born with the disorder and no mouth. They created one with a scalpel. He also had a weak heart, which the doctors repaired surgically. They discovered that his esophagus did not work properly either; it was something they suspected. He had spent much of his younger years on a gastronomy tube. Even now, he had to be careful with many foods. The rest of the articles were about his parents suing the doctor for a child that should never have been born. They had had to sell their house twice to cover medical costs and special treatments. Despite the child's resilience, his parents were asking for the right of the child to say, "I am a wrongful life." They had not been informed about the remote risks of cortical atrophy and mental retardation. The ultrasounds had revealed nothing, but both his parents, the papers reported, would have aborted the fetus had they known.

Ms. Cavenleigh looked at him, and he looked at her.

He knew he was ugly and difficult to look at. His eyes were dark and sunken; his eyebrows were crushed in toward his skull. His nose was broad, and one of his cheeks seemed pushed to one side. His hair was coarse, matted, and short. His skull had weird shapes that did not go together. His mouth was small, and although the skin around his mouth had been tattooed a natural color to make it look like lips, the ink seemed to have reacted with his skin and turned black. His chin was full and strong, but it only exaggerated his short neck. And as difficult as she found it to look at him, Tom thought, he saw how easy it was for her to look at Lawrence. This bothered him. Ms. Cavenleigh was attractive, which only made more urgent his curse: he liked everything beautiful. As he was ugly, he loved beauty; what could be more natural, he thought. As he was the ugliest, he loved the most beautiful, Eileen. As life would have it for him, she loved Lawrence.

He noticed Ms. Cavenleigh look in Lawrence's direction. She seemed hesitant, he thought, as if she did not want to discuss in class the poem he had chosen. Tom could feel himself becoming stiff and rigid. He noticed everyone staring at him like he really was the freak he appeared to be. He usually left class when everyone stared like this.

He stood to leave, but his legs would not move.

Ms. Cavenleigh turned away from Tom and walked to her desk to sit down.

"Tom, tell us, why does the Raven say 'Nevermore'?" she asked.

He stood straighter as he felt all eyes on him.

"BECAUSE LENORE IS DEAD."

The room seemed lifeless for a moment, and there was silence around him.

"Why does that translate into 'Nevermore'?" asked Ms. Cavenleigh.

"SHE WAS HIS LIGHT, NOW SHE IS DEAD."

He could see faces cringe around him, as if he had killed Lenore.

"And why can't his soul be lifted from the floor?" she asked.

"BECAUSE HE IS DEAD TOO."

"Why do you say that?" she asked, confused.

"BECAUSE HE KILLED HER. IT IS THE SAME."

He saw others looking scared, as if they would leave; this surprised him. He squinted his eyes.

"No, no. He's alive. Perhaps he will not want to live without his Lenore, but I don't think he killed her."

"HIS DARKNESS DID."

"No, no, I don't agree," she said softly. "But why does it seem that the death of one is like the death of the other?"

Tom watched her look around the classroom.

"Anyone?" she asked.

"BECAUSE ONE IS BUT THE SHADOW OF THE OTHER," he growled.

"What do you mean?" she asked.

Tom stood there thinking for a moment. One leg hurt from standing as straight as he could. And again he felt the weight of his classmates turning their gaze toward him. He hunched forward and put one hand out on his desk to hold himself still. He was excited, animated, nervous, and the room was moving. At this moment, he realized he had one problem: he was not really sure what he was trying to say. Nonetheless, he wanted to speak.

"I MEAN THAT . . ." He could feel himself going blank, as if his mind were deserting him. He looked at Ms. Cavenleigh for help, but she looked elsewhere. ". . . BECAUSE THE RAVEN IS SITTING AT HIS DOOR," he said quickly, "LIKE A DEMON THROWING HIS SHADOW ACROSS THE FLOOR. AS SHE WAS HIS LIGHT AND HOPE, HE IS HER DARKNESS. THE RAVEN IS HIS OWN SHADOW . . ."

"So quoth the Raven," said Lawrence.

There were suppressed giggles followed by a hushed silence.

Tom thought he saw Ms. Cavenleigh smirk for a moment. He wanted to walk out of the room, but his legs hurt. He could feel himself getting angry and flustered.

"THE RAVEN IS HIM, HIS DARK SIDE, AND HE KILLED HER," he said, attempting to collect his thoughts.

"He didn't kill her," snapped Lawrence. "She died, and he is empty without her."

"But why have the Raven repeat 'Nevermore' over and over?" Ms. Cavenleigh asked.

She looked around from behind her desk.

Lawrence said, "Who knows if there is even a bird in his chamber or—"

"BECAUSE THE RAVEN IS HIM, HIS DARK SIDE," Tom cut in.

Ms. Cavenleigh held up her hand for Tom to stop.

"Sit down please, Tom," she said.

Tom swallowed hard and sat down.

"What do you think, Lawrence? Why does the Raven say 'Nevermore'?"

"He just means that his life is covered in a shadow, a bitter, dark shadow. Maybe it's because Lenore is dead, if there was a Lenore, but we don't know that. He is just say— "

"NO! HOW CAN YOU SAY THERE IS NO EILEEN? HE KILLED HER. SHE WAS LIGHT, HE WAS DARKNESS—"

The class burst out in laughter.

"That's enough, everyone. That's enough, Tom," Ms. Cavenleigh said with a smile. "Let's settle down now. I believe Lawrence was speaking. Carry on, Lawrence."

"I DON'T THINK YOU SHOULD PLAY FAVOURITES," said Tom.

"Play favourites?" asked Ms. Cavenleigh, standing up and walking toward him.

Lawrence turned to say something to Tom but stopped.

"Why would I play favourites, young man?" asked Ms. Cavenleigh as she approached him.

Tom clenched his teeth together and grabbed his desk in desperation to hold himself still.

"Now, I think you owe the class an apology. Why on earth would you say such a thing?"

He felt the desk shaking beneath him as he held it tighter and with envious hate looked straight at Lawrence.

"CAUSE YOU SLEEP WITH HIM."

Ms. Cavenleigh, red-faced, turned one way, then the other, and then marched out of the room.

Eileen looked at Tom and then at Lawrence.

Tom was shaking.

"You stupid ass," yelled Lawrence.

He jumped up and charged toward Tom as others rose to their feet to stop him.

Tom tried to stand, but several boys pushed him back down. He felt hands grab him and had one thought: he had to get out of here.

"You stupid freak," Lawrence screamed.

Everyone seemed to be standing around them. Tom could feel his face flush with a bitter nervousness as arms from every direction held him and Lawrence apart.

"DAMN YOU ALL," Tom screamed.

"You stupid, ugly freak," screamed Lawrence.

"GODDAMN YOU. I KNOW I'M UGLY."

Tom's voice was an ominous sound.

Larry, Larry, Larry . . . What the hell are you doing? Lawrence asked himself.

He took a couple of steps back.

"I'm sorry," he said.

He looked at Tom as if he were looking at a dog hit by a car. Pity swept across his face.

Nothing made Lawrence more ugly in Tom's eyes.

Tom broke from the arms that held him and grabbed Lawrence by the throat. Lawrence didn't resist as Tom held him and violently yanked him to the floor, squeezing his neck tighter. Others tried to pull Tom off of him.

"ARRRRRGH," Tom groaned in hate.

Lawrence felt his throat collapsing as he tried to suck in air. He kicked and tried to throw Tom off.

Suddenly, Tom felt himself lifted from behind.

"What on earth are you doing?" screamed the vice principal as he grabbed Tom around the chest and pulled him off of Lawrence. For a moment he looked at Lawrence, then he shook Tom violently. "What on earth is wrong with you? You could seriously injure someone pulling stunts like this!"

While the vice principal held him, a fist came out of the crowd of bodies that surrounded him, and Tom felt it meet the side of his face. His brain seemed to burst into a million bits of light, then a grey darkness followed.

He was unconscious.

* * * * *

Eileen sat alone in the cafeteria. English class had been cancelled. She sat drinking a fruit juice, not sure how long she had been there. What Tom said about Lawrence was bothering her. Lawrence had looked so angry, and Tom had looked so alone.

She shook her head. "No, Lawrence is such a sweet guy," she said to herself. "Despite his anger, he apologized and didn't even try to fight back. Why would Tom say that, though?" She would ask him when she saw him, she told herself. But she wasn't sure she really wanted to. In her heart, she knew Lawrence—as well as most of the boys—liked Ms. Cavenleigh. And why shouldn't they? she thought. But that didn't mean they were sleeping with her.

"What a strange thing to say," she said aloud.

She looked around to see if anyone had heard her. Then she looked up at the clock; she was already late for gym class. She rushed to the changing room and undressed before realizing her tee shirt was in her locker. She threw back on her blouse and jeans and ran out into the hallway. As she turned the corner, she saw Tom standing at his locker. He turned in her direction, his eyes sad and lonely; his face was badly swollen. He had undergone a transformation, she thought. His ugliness was harsher, and his eyes seemed cold, as if he had further hardened himself against everything. She had never felt such pity for anyone in all her life.

She tried to smile, but she felt awkward with her sadness. She thought to wink at him that he might know some lighter kindness but was unsure of how he would take it. She felt pity and sadness for him yet did not want to look at him that way. Then, uncontrollably, she burst into tears.

Tom clenched his fists in front of himself and started to cry. As she walked over to him, he collapsed on the floor.

It was a terrible sight. His voice seemed muffled, as if it were encased in the cement of the floor as he cried. He looked badly injured. She didn't know what to do. She felt flustered and embarrassed. She stood there leaning over him, wanting to help him back to his feet as tears rolled down her face. She bent over him, put her hand to one side of his face, and kissed the top of his head. She didn't know that else to do.

She turned, went back to her locker, and then to the changing room.

Tom slowly rose to his feet. He emptied out his locker. With all his books in his arms, he rigidly pushed open the front door of the school and stepped outside.

He had been expelled.

He stood outside the front entrance for a moment and took a deep breath. Then, without looking back, he limped home.

* * * * *

When Tom arrived home, Aidan asked him what had happened.

"NOTHING," said Tom.

"Are you hurt?" asked Aidan.

"I'M FINE. I'M ALWAYS FINE."

Aidan sternly looked at him.

"I GOT IN A FIGHT AT SCHOOL."

Aidan offered to draw him a bath and make him something to eat, but Tom did not want to take a bath or eat. He went to his room. When Aidan checked on him shortly after, Tom was already asleep.

When Tom awoke in his room, the sun had not yet set, but

it was cloudy and getting dark. He got out of bed and stood at the window. He stood there waiting to wake up, pressing his swollen face against the cold glass, watching as it melted some of the frost. Seeing her in the hallway this afternoon with such concern for him had given him resolve. He would give Eileen the glasswork he had made for her. He went out to the shed and brought the piece to his room. He looked over at it and was struck by the sharp contrast between the roughly carved stone and the polished glass that covered three-quarters of it. He squinted, then leaned his head against it, resting his forehead against the body of the bird. He closed his eyes so that he would not let himself become too proud of it. After all, he was ugliest when smiling.

When it was dark enough, he wrapped a sheet around it, put it in a Christmas gift-bag, and left the house.

He walked slowly toward Eileen's house, as if giving himself time to reconsider. When he reached her house, he stood below the sun deck outside the sliding doors of her bedroom. He would leave the gift on the railing of the sun deck, he thought. She would see it when she woke up on Christmas morning, take it out of the bag, and then know what was inside of him.

He carefully felt it beneath the cloth as he quietly walked up the staircase of the sun deck. He angled the bag so that she would see it from her room. Then he left.

He did not look back as he walked away. He just kept walking until he reached the creek beyond her back yard. There, as if making a final salute, he turned and looked back toward her room. He noticed some flickering light from her bedroom window. He didn't know what it was at first. He waited for a moment, then slowly started walking back toward her house as the flickers grew brighter.

Her room is on fire, he thought.

Panic-stricken, he started to run. As he neared, he quickly saw that the flickers were just the glow of candles. Had she lit them in tribute? he asked himself tremulously. From the stairs, he caught a glimpse of her standing at the foot of her bed with something loose draped over her shoulders, and she was holding out her arms as if embracing the night.

Tom quietly climbed the remaining stairs and stepped toward the sliding doors. He thought to tap on the glass as he approached, but when he raised his hand, he saw Lawrence emerge from the shadows, stepping toward Eileen and putting his arms around her.

Tom stumbled backward for a moment and fell against the railing.

"WHAT DID YOU EXPECT?" he said to himself.

He clenched his fists and violently punched his own face. He stayed there for a moment and steadied himself against the railing, then pulled himself to his feet.

He grabbed the piece, descended the stairs, and ran.

* * * * *

At first Tom ran blindly. He did not think about where he was going until he reached the creek. Letting the creek decide for him, he followed its banks until he reached the flat bridge.

Why had he so naively thought that somehow she would like him? Had he made the piece with that intention in mind yet studiously never admitted it to himself? He realized now that it wasn't so special, and it wasn't even that good. He shook his head at how he thought this would make him less ugly . . . less of an eyesore . . . and that this would somehow make her like him.

He sat down on the bridge with his legs dangling over the side. He put his head down. He was not only ugly, he thought, he was a fool. He was an ugly, deformed boy who liked a beautiful girl. What could be more foolish than expecting that she would be blind enough to like him? She was a normal person, of course she would find him hideous. He was. No piece of glasswork could change that, he thought.

He sat there with his head down while shivering in the

cold. He finally stood up, holding his gift bag, and walked along the creek a little further to the point where the water widened and deepened. He stood there for a moment with a lowered head, then threw the bag out into the middle of the creek. It seemed to hang in the air for a moment, then, in almost complete silence, it was gone, disappearing into the water.

He watched the ripples for a moment.

"MERRY CHRISTMAS," he yelled in bitterness.

He looked up to the sky to see if there were any ravens above him. They should be here, he thought. But the sky held only the windblown flurries of the light snow that had started to fall. It was getting much colder.

He limped home as the snow started to gather on the ground.

* * * * *

Never had he been so nervous.

Lawrence watched Eileen as she lit candle after candle.

"You should tell her that Tom was right," he said to himself. "She told you she didn't believe it, you said nothing. Something's wrong with me."

He watched her closely as she continued to light several more candles. She put the matches down, and at the foot of her bed, she held out her arms to him. He tried to walk toward her calmly, but it was with a sense of uncertainty that he neared. He awkwardly pulled the shawl from her shoulders and held her tightly against him, but not without shaking.

There was a noise outside.

"What was that?" he said to her.

"Nothing," she said, not really hearing anything. "Maybe just the house adjusting . . . it's getting colder."

She held him to assure him, but he seemed distracted. She continued to press herself against him, and he leaned his face toward hers until their lips met, but he did not really kiss her. His lips pressed hers distractedly as he listened to the sounds of the night.

He was nervous and not accustomed to it. Normally, he tried not to care, and his practiced aloofness kept him calm. But he could not make himself feel aloof. He pressed his lips numbly to hers and leaned toward the bed until somehow they were lying beside each other. He could feel the perspiration running down his back and under his arms, and his hands were cold and wet.

"What was that?" he asked again, alarmed at a sound he thought he heard.

She shrugged.

"I thought I heard something," he said in nervous apology.

He lay there breathing lightly, listening to the sounds of the night, not willing to get too involved in kissing her because he was not able to relax. In this state he became conscious of every squeak the bed made when he moved. He stopped moving.

He imagined a dog before him with cold, alien, lifeless eyes of grey. It appeared poised, waiting to attack. He tried to stay perfectly still—

"No one will be home till after midnight mass," she said.

It was as though she hadn't spoken.

He listened more intently and kissed her with feigned interest.

Then he suddenly sat up, as if he heard something and was about to run.

"I don't hear anything," she said.

Then he thought he heard the front door open.

"Your parents," he whispered in a panic as he jumped up from the bed.

He threw on his clothes, put on his shoes, opened the sliding door of the sun deck, and jumped over the railing. Landing heavily on the ground below her bedroom, he put on his jacket and started running.

"Jesus Christ," he cursed into the cold night.

He ran along the creek until he felt nothing could catch him. He did not look back at the house, so he did not see Eileen standing on the sun deck in her bathrobe as she watched him run across the back yard toward the baseball park. She stood shaking her head in disbelief that he had run away.

When Lawrence stopped running, he took several deep breaths.

"I've got to change. I've got to do things differently," he said. "Look at yourself, Larry. How else will she ever love you? You have to change . . . become a better person . . . Jesus, tell her about Ms. Cavenleigh—do something, for Christ's sake."

Lawrence walked further along the creek, breathing easier, until he saw someone sitting on the bridge. He stopped and moved behind some trees, thinking he would have to go back and use the road in front of Eileen's house to cross the creek. He waited a couple of moments, then recognized Tom.

What is he doing here? he wondered.

Lawrence hid behind a tree as the snow fell more heavily around him and watched as Tom stood, holding something in his hands.

* * * * *

On Christmas morning Tom awoke early as the sky began to lighten. He rubbed his eyes and told himself to think only about the sunrise. The sky quickly became bright with reflected light from the snow. He waited for the sunrise as he did on most mornings, but he did not bother with his morning wish for a better day. In his heart, Christmas had always been a sad time, a lonely time; he tried not to think about it.

"CHRISTMAS," he said to explain his mood.

It was an ugly mood. Maybe he would just not get up today. Maybe he would just lie here not moving.

He could hear Aidan downstairs.

It was early. Aidan got up early every Christmas morning. It was a tradition. Presents were opened while having tea and biscuits. A turkey dinner followed shortly after midday. Sometimes Aidan liked to sit at the table for the entire afternoon, alone or with Tom, or on occasion with neighbors who stopped in. He ended his Christmas dinner with a plum pudding that had a strong brandy sauce. Then he would light a cigar and sip some scotch. That was his Christmas, he always said. "Don't give me anything, just join me for dinner, a drink, and a cigar," he would say to Tom.

Tom listened to Aidan down in the kitchen getting it all ready. He would have the fireplace roaring, the turkey would be in the oven already, and Aidan would be dressed up and wearing an apron over his shirt and tie. Tom could hear him whistling Christmas carols with every step.

Tom stayed in bed, letting himself fall in and out of sleep. He heard Aidan whistle and chatter to himself. At times it sounded as if an army of people were in the kitchen. Then Tom heard Aidan's knock at his bedroom door.

"May I come in?" he heard Aidan ask.

Tom didn't answer. He always struggled when someone was too happy in the morning. It just didn't seem right, especially on Christmas Day.

Aidan slowly opened the door and approached Tom with an extended hand.

"Merry Christmas, my son," he said.

He shook Tom's hand and bent toward Tom and hugged him. "Merry Christmas, Merry Christmas, Tom."

"MERRY CHRISTMAS," said Tom.

"I wouldn't normally be waking you this early, but we have a special guest joining us for morning tea and biscuits. As usual, I would be honored to have you join me. You'd best shower and clean up."

Aidan left as quietly as he had come. Tom stretched and slowly got out of bed to shower. So much for staying in bed, he thought.

He had never liked Christmas, he thought as he came down the stairs into the kitchen after his shower. He shook his head as he watched how excited Aidan got with putting out some jams and jellies on a tray.

"There's juice if you want, or you can wait for tea," said Aidan as he added teacups to the large serving tray.

"I'LL WAIT."

As the thought occurred to Tom that it was a little surprising that Aidan had asked one of the neighbors to join them, the doorbell rang.

"Answer the door . . ." said Aidan as he pulled the hot biscuits from the oven.

Tom limped to the door and opened it.

Eileen stood there.

Tom stood there looking at her.

"Merry Christmas, Tom," she said.

He continued looking at her without moving.

"May I come in?" she asked.

"Invite her in, Tom, for heaven's sake!" said Aidan.

"Thank you, Mr. Tyler," said Eileen as she stepped past Tom and came into the house. "Merry Christmas," she said.

"Merry Christmas," Aidan said, putting down the pan of hot biscuits. He went over to her and kissed her cheek. "Let me take your coat."

"This is for you. Dad told me you like this," she said, handing Aidan a bottle of scotch covered with a large bow. "And this is for you," she said, turning to Tom, handing him a small book with a bow on it. "It's nothing really," she said. "I at least wanted to thank you for inviting me for tea."

"Well, thank you for coming, and you didn't have to do this," said Aidan, putting the bottle of scotch on the kitchen counter.

Tom looked at the book.

"It's a collection of some poems by Edgar Allan Poe," she said. "Do you have it already?" she asked.

He shook his head.

"Come in, have a seat by the fire. May I pour you a cup of tea?" asked Aidan.

"Yes," she said.

"Well, I baked us some biscuits to go with our tea," he said.

He brought the plate of biscuits over and poured three cups of tea.

"I didn't get you anything, but I believe Tom has something for you," Aidan said, not looking at Tom.

Wide-eyed, Tom looked at Aidan and shook his head.

Aidan smiled at Eileen, then looked straight into Tom's eyes and said, "Why don't you go out to the shed and get it?"

"NO . . ." he protested.

Tom stood looking at Aidan in disbelief, shaking his head. Why me? What did I ever do? he asked himself.

"Well, why don't we all go out?" asked Aidan.

Tom stood shaking his head.

Aidan looked at Eileen. "Is it okay with you?" he asked.

"Sure . . ."

Aidan handed her back her coat, grabbed a sweater, and offered his arm to Eileen.

Tom grabbed Aidan's arm.

"It's quite okay, Tom," Aidan assured him. He led Eileen out the door, and Tom followed them, trying desperately to think of what he had made recently that he could give to her.

Aidan approached the shed and opened the door for Eileen to enter. Then he waited as Tom limped toward the shed. Tom looked harshly at Aidan as he entered. And out in the middle of the workstation, on the stone table, was a cloth draped over an object of some sort, with a bow stuck on top of it.

"Uncover it," said Aidan to Eileen.

Tom's heart sank as Eileen walked over to it. He wondered what Aidan could have possibly put there.

She pulled off the cloth.

Tom looked incredulously at Aidan. How did he get it? he asked himself.

Wide-eyed, Eileen walked around it.

"This . . ." she said slowly, looking at the bird-shaped piece of stone covered in glass. She gently touched it. ". . . Is this for me?" she asked.

She was mesmerized.

Tom nodded his head.

She started to cry.

"It's beautiful," she said, crying. "I don't know what to say . . ."

"Lawrence said he was supposed to give this to you last night on behalf of Tom," said Aidan, "but he reconsidered and thought Tom should give it to you himself. It was at the front door when I got up this morning."

"LAWRENCE?" asked Tom.

"Yes," said Aidan.

"I didn't really think you two were friends." said Eileen.

"WE'RE NOT," said Tom. He didn't say anything else.

Eileen continued looking at the gift.

"It's incredibly beautiful," she said. "I don't know how to thank you."

"I JUST WANTED . . . A FRIEND . . ." said Tom.

"You are my friend," said Eileen, and she kissed Tom's cheek. "Merry Christmas, Tom."

"MERRY CHRISTMAS," Tom whispered.

He tried to squint his eyes but couldn't. His heart asked him why it couldn't always be like this, and he started to cry.

"Don't worry," said Aidan, noticing Eileen's concern, "this is how he shows he is happy. For him it means this is a Merry Christmas."

Aidan smiled at Eileen, who was looking at the glass piece, and he smiled at Tom, who was wiping the tears from his face.

"What do you call this piece?" asked Eileen.

Tom tried to look at her.

"THE RAVEN," he said.

She was looking at it from one angle after another. "This is really for me?"

"YES."

"Tom McIntyre, what am I to do with you? You offer a friend so much."

He squinted his eyes and cried again.

She looked at Tom, and Tom raised his head to look at her.

"I'll be the best friend I can be," she said.

"ME TOO! I'LL WORK HARD. I PROMISE—" His voice broke off. "I WON'T BE STUPID," he finished.

"Neither will I, if I can help it," said Eileen.

Why couldn't all of life be like this? Tom thought. He tried to say thank you, he tried to say Merry Christmas, he tried to take her hand to shake it and thank her, but his body shook as if he were shivering, and the words wouldn't come out. His lips quivered, and the tears rolled down his cheeks as he squinted his eyes and cried.

Eileen took his arm.

"It's okay," she said to him, "it's okay. You just have to get used to this, that's all."

One Candelabrum

"Hello, hello," said Aunt Eli.

"Hello," I said, kissing her cheek.

My sister just nodded.

"I'm glad you both could come. I'll take your coats," she said in her crackling voice.

She politely ignored or didn't seem to notice my sister's snub.

My sister and I handed her our coats and waited in the entrance hall for her to return from the other room. It was a small apartment and smelled of peroxide, mulling spices, apple cider, and bad vinegar. When she returned, she led us to a small oval table in front of the living room window, and we sat down beside each other.

"May I offer you some hot cider?" she asked.

My sister sort of moved her head.

"Sure . . ." I said for both of us.

May as well have some if she already made it, I figured.

We had not visited our Aunt Eli before. She had visited us on a few occasions, but that was it. She was the oddball in my mother's family. She was fairly tall and a bit gangly. She had long grey hair that she braided and tightly wrapped around her head and held in place with bobby pins . . . serious bobby pins . . . lots of them. With a hat over it maybe it wouldn't have looked half bad, but she wasn't wearing a hat, and her hair was streaked yellow - who knows what she was probably using on her hair, maybe the peroxide I smelled. And the many ends that were too short to braid stuck out like little tails glued to the back of her head. Amongst relatives, rumor had it that her hair went down well past her ankles. All I can say is, there was enough there to believe it. She looked a lot older than Mom ever had. I guess some people wear well . . . others just age. She aged, I guess. A few more years and she would have looked more like my grandmother than my aunt. Mom died six years back. She was fifty-one years old, but she never approached looking as old as Aunt Eli, except right at the end when she was really sick. But some people just seem older, like they are from a different generation than everyone else their age. Maybe that was it with her. And really, I wasn't sure of what to expect. My sister Sally wasn't sure either.

My sister's name is Sarah, but she never liked it, even as a child, so we call her Sally. Old Sally can be a pain in the ass, though, I tell you. She never rethinks something once she's decided . . . kind of like my mom.

I looked at the sparse surroundings, the worn-out couch, and the tattered chairs. I nodded to old Sally and whispered, "Yucko!!"

The green tablecloth that covered the small oval table appeared new, but it looked like it was really a fitted bedsheet, although I couldn't see the elastic border. The white paint on the wall had faded to yellow, and there were many cracks in the drywall. The hardwood floor was a dirty caramel brown color, and in some areas the small pieces of hardwood were missing. What I could see of the kitchen looked worse than the living room.

But Aunt Eli was an oddball, so what the hell did any of it mean? Maybe she was rich and stashed it all away. We didn't know. Or at least I didn't know. She lived alone. Always had. She was older than my mom by three years, but frankly, that was all I really knew. Conversations about her were taboo in our house, I'll tell you that. Mom and Dad didn't talk about her, nor did they encourage us to, even as we got older. Sally just kind of freaked out when old Aunt Eli was even mentioned. Oh well. The only thing I can say is that the few times I met her, she looked at me as if she were looking into the past, the future, or somewhere else. I was never sure she even knew I was there, if you know what I mean. So she could be odd in that way at least.

She had contacted us, not Dad, when Mom died . . . and this year she asked if we would visit at Christmastime . . . She had something she wanted to give us. I mean, my sister hated her, but I didn't know why, and I'm not sure she knew why. Just one of those things, you know. For those like her who knew, no explanation was necessary. For those like me who didn't, none was possible. But old Aunt Eli didn't seem that bad to me. I probably should have come here alone. I mean, old Sally came along because I told her I was going. Maybe she thought she could protect me were something ugly to happen. Besides, I didn't want to walk, so I needed a ride or someone with a license to drive with me. Being older and having her driver's license, Sally liked to think she was teaching me how to drive, even though she was a lousy driver. I already regretted her coming. She was sitting there, looking like she was going to be a dick. It was probably partly my fault; I wasn't doing so well in her books. Says I ruined her chance to date some hot guy at school because I made an idiot out of myself. Actually, I jokingly told this guy that Sally had done the high school guidance counsellor - it isn't a pretty thought - and somehow she found out what I said. I was just joking around, but I guess this guy thought funny things about old Sally after that. Idiot has been her favorite name for me since. The way I figure it, if this guy as a senior in her class was too thick to figure something like that out, then I did her a favor. But I guess she really liked him or something.

Anyway, enough of that.

To be fair to old Aunt Eli, she just looked like a normal old woman to me - a little older and more worn than many, but a lot like my mom. Maybe she was okay-looking when she was younger. It's hard to tell with old people. They all look the same really. And plus, they do funny stuff with their hair. It's like, poof . . . they've walked out of a wind tunnel. Aunt Eli's was a little different. More like, zappo . . . it's a woven helmet.

"Let me know if you find it too cold. I'll turn up the radiators," she said. She handed us our hot cider from a tray and put one on the table for herself. "These walls are not well insulated. My heating bills are horrendous." She sat down and seemed to clasp the cup in her hands for heat. The window was mostly frosted over, and when she lit the five candles on the table, she pushed them toward it. She left all the lights on, though; not much of an atmosphere.

"I hope you will forgive me for saying so, but Christmas is an odd time of year for me," she said. "I long for it because it makes me sad. Sometimes I want to be sad. It's a peculiar thing, I grant you, for someone as old as me." She lifted a small plate of cranberry-orange bread and offered it to us. Neither of us accepted. "Help yourself should you change your mind."

She pushed one of the candles on the table even closer to the window.

Now that I had my coat off, it was a little cold in here.

"Perhaps we shall be fortunate this evening and the candles will melt some of the frost on this window. One of my few pleasures regarding Christmas is to see the snowflakes fall, especially on Christmas Eve. I always sit here with candles close to the window to melt away the frost.

"My Great-aunt Sarah got us lighting candles when we were young. But maybe we were too young to understand exactly what she was trying to tell us. Warnings are so easy to dismiss, so easy to disregard. I think we both shrugged, as sisters often do, and we probably giggled. I would not shrug or giggle today . . . nor would your mother, I should think . . .

"So, I asked you to come tonight because I wanted to tell you about our Great-aunt Sarah. She was someone your mother and I both loved deeply. But first I must tell you that I loved your mother more than I loved anyone . . ."

She looked at the both of us like she was about to say something unbelievable.

"My hair was not always white, you know. At one time men found me attractive . . . and a little brash. I did have a spark, an attractiveness of sorts, and the boys sure made a fuss over me, as they did over your mother . . . She was a comely woman. We thought flirting with the boys was all for fun until we each fell in love. I chose not to marry. I had offers I didn't want, but that is another matter. Your mother had many suitors and interested parties before your father, but she met, fell in love with, and married your father, of course. And they spent many years together before having the two of you.

"The bread is still warm, please have some; it does so remind me of Christmas. When I was young, we spent our Christmas holidays at my Great-aunt Sarah's, and she always made cranberry-orange bread."

I took a piece as she lifted the plate toward us. Sally didn't. I guess she was just not in the visiting mood.

"You were named after our Great-aunt Sarah," Aunt Eli said to her. "It's such a lovely name."

I thought for sure Sally would lecture her on how she didn't like the name, how the name made her sick to her stomach and gave her cramps or something - and that her name was Sally. But old Sally didn't say boo.

"Our Great-aunt Sarah lived out in the middle of nowhere in the plains of the Midwest," Aunt Eli continued. "The winters were cold, a dry cold we never knew in our small town. Your mom, Wendy May, and I loved visiting relatives and spending Christmas at our Great-aunt Sarah's. Our two brothers didn't like it; they always seemed to be leaving girlfriends behind. But for Wendy May and me, a part of the reason we liked going was that it was the only opportunity we had to see any fellas besides our brothers. It is true that many of them were our cousins or related, but we didn't much concern ourselves with that so long as we saw boys we could flirt with. Even from a young age, your mother was a first-class flirt . . . I was no slouch myself . . . And my, we were cruel to the boys who liked us back then, both of us. We would get our cousins fighting over us and running around like ducks looking for bread whenever we were visiting. We spent all of our time, morning and afternoon, flirting with these boys. My, by evening they would all be prancing up a storm. Their fathers would come down on them pretty hard by the time dinner was ready, what with all the fuss they would be making against each other. But we always agreed to circumvent any of their attempts at stealing our hearts. We were cold, heartless flirts of the most frustrating kind. We spent every evening at Great-aunt Sarah's, getting her to tell us stories that we would intently listen to. Great-aunt Sarah loved her stories. It would drive all the boys beyond distraction. When clean-up was finished and she put her large pot of tea over the fire, that was the signal stories were about to be told, and anyone not appreciating her voice would be wise to leave. It was always a point of conflict for the fellas. Should they stay and hope to win more of our attention? Or should they just cut their loses and call it quits?

"Great-aunt Sarah lived in a large, grey brick house. It was a simple, box-shaped house with a sharp, sloping roof. The brick was a weatherworn grey and brown, and you had to duck through a small barn-wood door to get in. The house was divided into small room after small room with doorway after doorway that seemed to weave through the house, ending at the dining room and fireplace. The windows were small and did not allow much light in. But keeping the cold out was more of a concern than letting the light in, so Great-aunt Sarah's house was always dark, but usually warm. The windows had been put in at knee height, so adults had to stoop down to look out. And there was something desolate about her place. It sat at the top of a hill, and there was nothing near it. There were no trees or fences close by, and even the garden and the barn were at the bottom of the hill. The place left you feeling close to heaven and God, primarily because there was nothing else around.

"Over the years, Wendy May and I started to see less of our Great-aunt Sarah, although as children we loved her stories and believed them heart and soul. Compared to ours, her life was full of excitement, like the adventurers in the books we read. Her and her sister hunted - they each had their own rifle - and they had had many encounters with wild animals and poisonous snakes. They had fought off black bears trying to take their blueberries, bobcats trying to take their rabbits, and they once had to escape the clutches of a grizzly bear. They had been stopped by bandits, were trained in Indian tracking methods, knew pioneers as friends, did some panning for gold - ah, we prayed to live that kind of life. It seemed so exciting.

"I don't remember exactly how old Wendy May and I were when Great-aunt Sarah pulled us aside. It was in the spring; maybe I was seventeen or even eighteen."

* * * * *

She looked at us and pointed her cane upstairs.

She had always had a bad leg, so we helped her up the steep stairs of the old farmhouse, into the room in the attic that we used when we were staying there. She went to the closet.

She pointed her cane toward the bed.

We went over and sat on the bed. She pulled the closet curtains open and took out an old, dusty, black-and-green hatbox. Then she limped her way toward us. It was obvious that she was going to sit between us, so we quickly made room on the small bed as she turned her backside toward us and plopped down.

After catching her breath, she straightened out her bad leg, closed her eyes for a moment, and slowly began.

"I have been waiting to give you something," she said, "but I wanted to tell you something first. It is something no one told me when I was young, yet I have often wished someone had. And it is this: You must cherish your friendships, both of you, for when you get to be old like me, somehow it's the cherishing that matters most. Most of us don't realize that until it is too late." She took a deep breath. "Well, where to begin? Oh, goodness, I wanted to show you something first. This is the wrong box."

She put the hatbox down, made her way back to the closet, and returned to the bed with a large dirty shoebox. She put
in on her lap and sadly smiled. She wiped it off, then set the lid
aside. Then she shuffled through bundles of black-and-white
photographs that were kept together with various pieces of ribbon. She finally found the bundle she seemed to be searching
for.

But once she looked at several of the photographs, she
said, "No, this isn't it," and started digging through the box
again. After a few attempts, she did find the photograph she was
looking for.

"Now close your eyes," she said. "Keep them closed until I
say to open them. Do you remember when I gave you those old
cowboy hats for Christmas quite a few years back? One brown,
the other black? You both wore them around the whole time you
were here? Remember? Well, open your eyes," she said.

Eli and Wendy May opened their eyes, and their Great-aunt
Sarah held up a photograph of two young girls wearing cowboy
hats.

"It's so old," Eli said.

"That can't be us," said Wendy May.

Great-aunt Sarah laughed.

"It isn't," she said. "It's me and your grandmother, my sister, Ava. She would have been pleased to know you wore our
hats. When we were young, those hats were our pride and joy.
We loved them and wore them everywhere."

The girls sat looking at it, awestruck. They looked at each
other, then down at the photograph, then at their Great-aunt
Sarah.

"It's the only photograph I have of us wearing our hats,"
she said. "See, you look much like we looked. We were insepa-
rable too. But unlike you two, we had a difficult childhood. Oh,
I know you don't want to be hearing about how good you have
it, but I'm not telling you this because of that. I just want to tell
you to cherish what you have. Ava died a few years after your
mother was born, and I never knew how much she was a part of

me till she was gone. Ava was my older sister, my best friend, and my teacher. I'm at a loss to explain even now how often she carried me on her shoulders, in her arms, and on her back, always lifting me, coaxing me, looking after me because I wasn't able to look after myself. I've had this bad leg since childhood, and Ava was often the legs I didn't have. Although my leg has gotten worse again, it is still not anything like it was when I was young." She sighed sadly. "But where to start," she said as she paused to breathe and compose herself.

Her memories meant more to her than anything else.

"Don't remember my father," she told them. "One day he simply walked out of the house when I was three, and me and my sister never saw him again. A couple of years after that, in an accident, Mother was kicked by a horse. I think Ava was nine and I was five. For three weeks our mother fought to live, but she didn't win that battle. Apparently, our mother's sisters could not afford to take both of us. They were going to split us up, but Ava insisted on us staying together. Everybody was struggling back then. Nobody wanted us, and it was simply a matter of who felt the worst about letting us starve in the street. Back then, you have to understand, most folks were poor, and it was accepted that some people would go without food. Beyond eating, there was only one thing a child didn't want to have to worry about: you did not want to be an orphan. It's difficult to explain today the attitude of folks toward orphans back then, what it meant and all. We didn't really understand what it meant to lose our mother until we did. Then we were out on the street. No food, no bed, no clothes other than what we were wearing, and people no longer called us by name. We were orphan children.

"I should tell you that I was never a strong girl. I had a bad leg from an accident when I was a baby. I don't remember any of it. Walking for me was an excruciating effort. I was slow and embarrassed by my physical defect. If I got tired, it was all I could do to drag my leg along behind me. After they buried my mother beside the church, Ava went from door to door for food. She asked for food and if anyone could take us in. The few who even considered it on accounts that maybe we could do farm work shut their doors to us once they saw me. They did not want to take on a crippled orphan child.

"I don't remember how long we lived in the streets. I do remember Ava trying to catch squirrels barehanded so that we wouldn't starve, and I remember her hands bleeding all the time from bites. I remember I was cold; the ground was frozen solid, and we spent all of our time simply trying to get enough food to make it through each day and stay warm. Ava would find a sheltered spot where I could stay to keep warm while she went begging for food. Eventually, a poor family in town took us in.

"When you have been out in the streets, every house looks like heaven's blessing. We wept that first night for the joy of sleeping on a cold dirt floor near a fireplace. And although they had a reputation for meanness, they were kind to us. Mind you, there was not much food, and the only meat was from the squirrels Ava would catch. They were poor, and soon after taking us on, the head of the household, who was either the father or the eldest son, took a disliking to us. We knew something was up when he started yelling that he could not feed the entire town and that he had his own to worry about. He had not been able to get work for over a week. Suddenly, we were a threat to what little food they had. No one can like you and turn you out to the streets in winter, so they quickly learned to dislike us. Then, in anger, they turned us out. That was three weeks before Christmas, and we were still in tattered summer clothes, with no shoes.

"Given all that we went through, I remember the hunger most. The cold just seemed to come from inside of us, and we were so numb most days that we stopped feeling it. But the hunger pains never went away. Yet somehow Ava came up with enough scraps to keep us alive. The town kids would call us 'orphan scallywags.' They even had a terrible song they would sing when we were around, a version of ring-around-the-rosy . . . as if we had the plague. I would cry while Ava chased most of them away. Some small boys threw chicken manure at us one day. I just cried and cried and didn't even wipe it off. I was losing all my feeling to the cold, and I was numb. I could barely walk, but Ava put me on her back and carried me around, and we begged for food at each door and hunted for scraps in the garbage when Ava could not catch any squirrels.

"Some children took to throwing stones at us to keep us away from their homes, and a rumour started in town that we had typhus. No one would go near us, and people sent their dogs out to chase us away. I was sure that we would die. But Ava never stopped trying. I was useless to her, but she carried me everywhere. And she came up with new ideas every day it seemed. She started roaming the countryside, asking farmers if they would take us in. She would walk from place to place until late in the afternoon, and when she returned, she would find yet a different place for us to stay, to shelter us from the approaching cold of night. Sometimes we would stay beneath the church, other times in a vacated doghouse, and once in a warm manure pile. Always, Ava tried to keep me warm, protecting me from the wind, the snow, and the cold as best she could, holding me, wrapping me up in her arms and breathing on my hands and face to keep me warm.

"That Christmas, death struck the town, as it did in those days, and quite a few people died. By Christmas Eve, we were not only freezing cold, but the food scraps were fewer and fewer, and for the first time, Ava looked as if she too had seen death, and it was coming for us. Christmas Day I would not get up because I thought we would die.

"I was always so weak in such situations. Always a burden . . ."

She put her hands over her eyes for a moment.

* * * * *

"We won't die," said Ava confidently.

She picked me up and carried me to the church. We crawled beneath it to get out of the wind. That was the last of what I remember really. I was underneath the floor of the church, in the crawl space beneath the floorboards, and I was as cold as ever. I remember we seemed to stay there for a long time. I fell in and out of consciousness or sleep, I don't know which. I was so weak, so tired, and so hungry, I could not even keep my head up. It was the only time in my life I was too weak to cry. I could hear songs sung by angels from above, but it was as if they were mumbled under water. I ached all over, and I vaguely remember wishing Saint Nicholas would bring us food.

When I came to, I didn't know where I was. My only salvation seemed to be that I recognized Ava as she forced stale, bitter-tasting popcorn into my mouth. I was choking and I was terrified. We were at the front of the nave, near the altar, lying on the wooden floor beside the Christmas tree. Our mother had always taken us into the church to see the Christmas tree, and Ava had carried me there and was pulling down more of the stringed popcorn decorations. She had been forcing the stale popcorn into my mouth, and I could feel my head spinning. She shook me and made me eat more, even though I really didn't want any. I started to cough. Then we heard some noise, and Ava pulled me underneath the pews, but the noise faded. When we came up between a different row, I saw an old white-haired woman, who was asleep.

"I wonder if Saint Nicholas sent her to us," I said to Ava.

"Shhh - " she hushed.

The old woman awoke. Ava grabbed hold of me, set to run, but the old woman looked at us as if she too were starving and homeless.

"I won't hurt you," she said to us weakly.

I could tell that Ava was still ready to run because she held me back when I tried to draw nearer to the old woman.

"I won't hurt you," she said again. "Where are your folks?"

Ava held me still.

"Your mother and father. Where are your mother and father?"

"We have no mother or father," I said. Then I couldn't help it. I started to cry.

"That's okay, dearie, that's okay," she said.

I took a couple of steps toward her because I liked her.

"Where do you live?" she asked us.

"Nowhere," I said. "Did Saint Nicholas send you?"

"I'm thinking that maybe he did," said the woman casually. Then she became quiet and tried to straighten herself up. "What are your names?"

"I'm Sarah, and this is my sister, Ava."

"You have nice names."

I smiled at her.

She looked around. "I guess mass is over," she said. "Did you see the Christmas tree when the candles were lighted?"

I shook my head.

She stood and walked toward the tree. She felt her pockets for matches but did not find any. Then she saw the popcorn on the floor and looked back at us. I thought we were in trouble.

"You poor dears," she said as if she were about to cry.

"It's okay," I said, "we didn't eat all of it."

She looked at us, smiled, and shook her head.

I walked to her side and she took my hand and kissed me on the head.

"Come," she said as she wiped her eyes, "let's have a look at this nice tree, the decorations, the pretty silk, the foil. Smell the pine. Can you smell it? Do you like it? It is so nice with all the candles lighted."

I sniffed the tree and looked at it.

"It's beautiful," I said.

"It is," said the old woman. "Come on." And she held out her hands to us and even Ava took one. She led us over to the drugstore and ordered warm milk and cookies for us. I almost fainted when I put my nose over the cup of warm milk. I drank it so fast that it burnt my mouth from the tip of my tongue to the back of my throat, but all I felt was a swirling dizziness.

She ordered us more.

"Not so quickly," she said.

I couldn't help it, I drank and ate as fast as I could.

Then she asked the clerk if she could speak with him, and in my dizziness I was sure she'd be telling him about the popcorn. But when she came back, she nicely asked us if we felt better. I was too dizzy and faint to answer, but I think Ava said something.

"Would you two like to live with me in my home?"

"Yes," I yelled, drunk on the warm milk.

"And you?" she asked Ava.

"We're orphans, madam," said Ava.

"I know that."

"You wouldn't split us up?" asked Ava.

"No, I wouldn't."

Ava looked at me and I looked at the old woman.

"Yes, ma'am, we would," I yelled and awkwardly spun in pirouettes, shouting, "We're going home, we're going home . . ."

"Then we'll have to take the next train out of this town. You may stay with me as long as you abide by two rules: You mustn't lie and you mustn't steal. Will you be able to abide by that?"

"Yes," I yelled.

"We'll get you tickets and maybe some clothes. What do you say?"

"She is Saint Nicholas," I screamed. I couldn't resist; I awkwardly spun around again and yelled as loud as I could, "Told you so, told you so . . ."

And so she adopted us as her own. She did everything for us, bought us clothes, food, put us in school, but she was not rich. She had lost her husband over the past summer and was unprepared to spend Christmas without him. She had been wandering aimlessly from town to town until she ended up exhausted. She went to the church because she was lonely and fell asleep during mass.

That Christmas when she took us home was the first time in our lives that Ava and I received a gift for Christmas. Till then, Christmas had always been a time when Saint Nicholas helped make sure we had something to eat. Our new mother gave us our first gift and left it under our first Christmas tree. She gave us each a beautiful candelabrum that her husband had bought for her as a wedding present. And every year she would buy us special candles for it, and we would light them together on Christmas Eve.

* * * * *

"I'm at a loss to explain what it all means to me . . ."

Slowly she got up from the bed and grabbed the large hatbox.

"I'm getting older now," said their Great-aunt Sarah, "and I'd like you girls to have these so that you will remember to cherish your friendship, both of you, for when you get to be old like me, somehow it's the cherishing that seems to matter most. Sometimes we don't find that out until it is too late. Now go ahead, take a look at them."

Eli and Wendy May pulled out the candelabrums. They looked at each other, and their Great-aunt Sarah put her arms around them.

"They're beautiful," they said.

"Merry Christmas, Eli, Merry Christmas, Wendy May. Now, you must remember to light your candles each Christmas Eve, and you must light them for the sake of the love you have for each other. Then in spirit that love will live on. Do you think you can both do that?"

They both solemnly nodded their heads.

* * * * *

"I still nod my head, much the same way," said Aunt Eli. "Great-aunt Sarah told us they were over one hundred years old.

"Maybe we were too young to understand what we were looking at. She told us that the base was a tree stump to represent living on earth, that the rough brass was shaped like bark and molded into faces to mean shared salt, that as the faces got closer to the top and the rough brass became smoother, the human shapes became two angels who look up to the heavens . . . and they open their wings in a semicircle behind them - this was to represent friendship and love. And she told us that the open wings hold five candles each, but only when put together so that the wings meet do the candelabrums hold two more to form a circle of twelve candles, or stars, which was to represent an entrance to the heavens above . . .

"Our Great-aunt Sarah passed away that summer. The following Christmas was a sad one, but we lit our candles for the love of each other, and although we didn't say it aloud, we lit them for the love we had for our Great-aunt Sarah, and the memory of her sister Ava, your great-grandmother.

"But I have been alone this Christmas as I have been alone for many Christmases. Each year I buy twelve special candles, and I light five of them by my window. I always hoped the two of us would find each other again on Christmas Eve, so I lit them for the love of my sister, Wendy May.

"Years, distance, and my foolishness separated us. There are some things that cannot be undone. I loved a man your mother cared for deeply, and he loved your mother . . . and he loved me too . . . I never told your mother. She found out. That was wrong . . . but it was many, many years ago, long before you two came into the world . . . long before your father . . . We were young, and he was young. In my heart I meant Wendy May no harm, but I sure hurt her. She forgave him, but she really didn't forgive me. But then, I was bitter about it too . . . him having promised himself and all . . . Boyfriends come and go, but I only ever loved him, even after all these years.

"It was a bitter wind in my heart, perhaps less bitter in your mother's heart. I know she found happiness and that your father and you two are part of the reason for it. I just wanted you both to know that I love your mother as I have loved so few in my life. And somehow it is the cherishing that seems to matter as you get older. That special cherishing of the sacred few who matter most to each of us.

"So this year I did not use my candelabrum because I wish to give it to you as a way of making amends. They are meant as a pair. Take it . . . both of you. But promise yourselves that on Christmas Eve you will try to light these candles in a spirit of love. And I hope that somehow their light may reach out to my sister, your mother, so she might understand that I have never forgotten our love - not for a moment - and that I love her more now than ever. And it is her love I cherish most. It is my hope that the two of you will someday know and cherish the love my sister and I have had for each other . . ."

She went quiet.

"Sure," I whispered. "Mom wanted Sally - Sarah . . . to have the candelabrum. Dad lights the candles on Christmas Eve, just like Mom used to every year."

I looked at Sally; she was looking bitter and wasn't warming to Aunt Eli. She sat as if she hadn't heard a word. I looked at Aunt Eli. She was gently nodding her head, and it seemed to me she was even sadder now. Maybe she had noticed Sally's blank expression.

I'm not sure how long we stayed. The candles seemed to melt some of the frost on the window, and in silence we all stared out into the night of winter. Old Aunt Eli really didn't have lots to say after that.

We left when the candles were burning down and the flickering yellow light made the room seem warm and maybe even friendly.

"Merry Christmas, Aunt Eli," I said, rising to my feet, "and thank you so much. It is a beautiful candelabrum."

She hardly moved at first. She seemed determined to sit there all night, as if she could see through the frost, through time, and to another place when she and Mom had been together.

She looked up and noticed me, then got up, put the candelabrum in a well-used shopping bag, and got our coats.

"Merry Christmas," she said, seeing us to the door.

"Merry Christmas," I answered.

Old Sally did the head-nod thing.

I kissed Aunt Eli's cheek and hugged her. I wanted to say something nice, that Mom thought of her, mentioned her, talked about her all the time, loved her . . . nice things. But then, I didn't know, and I was sure Sally would jump all over whatever I said.

I picked up the candelabrum and stepped out into the cold wind.

"She's nice," I said, feeling Sally had been unfair. "She really loved Mom."

Sally moaned.

Before we got to the car, I looked back, and I could see her sitting at the window, watching the night, the snowflakes, and maybe the memories of Mom beyond her window.

I shook my head in sadness. It was too bad she was alone.

"What are you shaking your head about?" Sally asked coarsely.

"She seems nice. She must be awfully lonely."

"You are so naive. It's all bullshit."

"How can you say that?"

"Because it's true."

"So, let's say it is. Let's have her over."

"You're an idiot."

I didn't say anything for a couple of moments. I got into the car, unlocked Sally's door, started the engine, and took out the brush and scraper to clear the windows. The snow was starting to come down, even though it was really cold.

When I got back in the car, Sally seemed better.

"I thought Mom said that Dad was her only boyfriend," I said to make conversation.

"He was," snapped Sally.

Maybe she wasn't okay.

"Well, how can that be?" I asked.

"How can what be?"

"Aunt Eli said that she loved the same guy Mom was dating before Dad, and that he loved her."

"It was Dad, you idiot. Now let's get the hell out of here."

"Dad?" I said.

"Put the damn car in gear and let's go."

"Dad? You mean, it was Dad she was talking about?"

"Are you always so quick?"

"Some days," I responded.

I put the car in gear and backed out of the driveway.

"Well, we should get Aunt Eli over for sure then."

"You really are an idiot."

I thought I should let it go at that.

I drove and looked out at the falling snowflakes.

"It's a beautiful candelabrum. It's got to be over one hundred and fifty years old. It's neat that the tips of the wings are designed to touch and form a circle between the two angels."

Sally didn't say anything.

"Merry Christmas, Aunt Eli and Wendy May . . ." I said.

We drove in silence.

The snow was falling more heavily, and I had to drive a bit slower.

Maybe I'll talk to Dad about having her over; it's time for him to get on with things. Mom passed away, but we all can't sit around like dicks. We'd just have to be careful not to tell old Sally. She could be an old hag. She's more like Mom than I realized. I love my mom, but she was some stubborn with things, may she rest in peace.

"Sally . . ." I said.

What the hell, I figured, may as well piss her off to the moon.

She looked over at me.

"What do you think of having Aunt Eli join us for Christmas dinner tomorrow night?"

I like doing that to old Sally. Watch her blow off a bit - get pissed   and see how it goes from there.

What the hell, it's Christmas . . . and it comes but once a year.

Fah Who

"Everything's fine," she whispered to herself.

She turned the old Pontiac Parisenne into the long driveway and pulled to the side of their farmhouse. She put the gearshift into Park.

"Everything's just fine."

She sat back in her seat and slowly closed her eyes to give herself a moment. She took a deep breath, then she puckered her lips and kissed the air. Slowly, she raised her knees. In her mind she tried to put a face on the man who would someday open the door of her car and sit beside her. Without a word, he would kiss her lips and press her against the seat. He would hold her there with confidence and certainty as he unbuttoned her blouse and removed her skirt. He would pepper her face and neck with kisses, then he would press her forcibly against the car seat till it hurt. She would love that pain and would hold him as passionately as she could, releasing her desire to his lips, hands, and legs.

She held herself in that position for a moment longer, then with resignation lowered her knees and pulled her coat back down.

She blankly stared at her elevated home, which was sitting on two long, rusty I-beams of steel.

For years she had complained mildly to Peter about the condition of their home. Each spring when the temperatures rose and the ground thawed, the melted snow ran toward the house, making it an island surrounded by mud and water. For two months they placed boards across the mud to be able to walk to and from the house. Some years, the boards sank and weren't seen for weeks. As well, an old barnlike shed had been attached to one side of the house. The shed had become home for some of the livestock they had. Each spring the mud and water covered the floor of the shed, and the livestock could be smelled from inside the house. This past summer, Peter had moved the livestock to the barn in order to tear down the shed and relocate the house away from the basin. He removed the windows and boarded the frames and did the same with the doors, except the one at the back. Then, on the first weekend in July, he had a friend in construction and some neighbors help him raise the house onto the large, thick I-beams of steel that ran the length of the structure. It had taken almost all day to hoist the house onto the I-beams. The beer was brought out, and that was the end of it. They never got around to digging a foundation for its new location.

Over the rest of the summer, she had put the windows back in. When the cold, mid-October winds blew, she resigned herself to the state of their home and used planks of wood to board up the space beneath the house and the frozen ground to try and keep the house warm. But the house was forever cold. With the shed removed, it was even colder. The exposed wall made the house cold, even on the mildest days. The brickwork had not made it through the lifting and hoisting without cracking, and in one corner, a space in the brickwork was large enough to see through. One of the children had poked a woolly sock of Peter's into it to plug it. In the wind, the faded grey sock with its red heel flapped around the corner of the house from side to side.

"Everything's just fine, really," she whispered as she looked at the sock.

She looked around at the house and the farm and thought it seemed nicer with the snow covering it. The roof looked clean and white, the mud and dirt of the yard were hidden, and the snow stuck to the weatherworn brick. It was a large, two-storey orange-brick farmhouse with high, sharp peaks on each facing. It felt less and less like home, though . . . even with the children, she thought.

As a mother, she was disgusted with herself for such thoughts, but she was tired of convincing herself of what she should feel rather than admitting what was true. She wasn't a proper mother, and she didn't live in a proper house, and nothing in her life was right. This had never been the home she wanted, nor had she married a man she wanted, nor was she the woman she wanted to be. If she had been born ten years later, or not in a small town in the Midwestern countryside, none of this would have happened. Today, just about anywhere, waiting would have been the thing to do.

She looked away from the house. On the other side of the long driveway was a row of large cedars that Peter had transplanted years ago to shelter the driveway from the blowing wind. But he had put them on only one side. The row of cedars helped snowdrifts develop across the driveway and front yard. Once the snow built up against the cedars, it extended into drifts fifty yards back. They had been putting up snow fences along the other side of the driveway since. She looked at the fields beyond and the blowing snow sweeping across and piling up at the snow fences. All of it would melt come spring and surround the house.

It is always so desolate and depressing here, she thought.

She closed her eyes, took a deep breath, and found the strength to turn off the car. She opened the door, got out, reached across the torn seat for the two bags of groceries, lifted them into her arms, one after the other, then shut the car door with her foot. She trudged along the path and up the icy blocks of wood to the door that was the only accessible entrance. She pushed the door open, stepped inside, and put her groceries down on a bench Peter insisted be just inside the crowded doorway. She sat on the bench and took off her heavy galoshes. She knew everyone would be out. It was the afternoon of Christmas Eve. She rubbed her hands together from the cold and quickly put a couple of logs into the wood-burning stove in the far corner of the kitchen. She hated the cold.

She put away the groceries, took a couple of meat pies from the freezer, and put them into the oven. She would serve meat pie and hot chocolate when everyone returned. Peter would have the children out chopping down their Christmas tree and then tobogganing in Hughes Valley. They had to go all the way to the valley to get a tree anyway, so Peter would toboggan with them there until everyone was hungry. After meat pie and hot chocolate, together as a family they would decorate the tree and sing Christmas carols.

When the kitchen warmed a little, she took off her coat.

She went upstairs, started her bath water, and scattered bath crystals into the tub. The crystals foamed and made the water blue. She left the bath running and glanced in her bedroom mirror as she walked by it. In front of the mirror, she took off her clothes and put on a thick bathrobe. She tried to remember when she had last taken a good look at herself. She opened her robe. She was a little flabby in spots, she thought. Her large breasts never did regain their firmness after her youngest was born, but the bones in her shoulders that made her look a little gangly when she was younger were no longer prominent. At forty-two years of age, she thought she still looked okay.

She took a few moments more to look at herself in the mirror as goosebumps covered her flesh and made her pale skin appear blue. She wrapped her bathrobe around herself and returned to the bathroom. She lit three candles around the large tub. Then she sat on the edge of the tub and looked out the small window, waiting for the water to rise.

Her bath was her Christmas. Everything else this time of year was a tolling bell of duty that rang from her eardrums to her breast. But this was for her, no one else. Once a year, for a few precious moments, she would sit in a tub of warm water and think about how Christmas ought to be. She would dream, fantasize, and make wishes . . .

She looked down at the tiger paws of the tub. The head of the tub was centered against one wall, which left space around three sides of it. The hardwood floors were in good shape, and the walls weren't cracked. A dark cherry wood lined the lower half of the room, and she had painted the walls above a dark aqua green. No one used this bathroom or the tub; it was her room. They all used the bath and shower in the other washroom. She had never asked them not to use it. She suspected Peter had told them not to; he could be a good man that way.

When the water rose to the level of the chain and the plug, she shut the tap off and dropped her bathrobe onto the floor. With one knee down on her bathrobe, she closed her eyes and lowered her head.

"Merry Christmas, Nancy," she whispered to herself.

She knelt for a moment longer and took a deep breath. She looked at the flames of the candles. She secretly hoped that someone would rescue her today. The candles seemed to flicker with her wish, as if someone had opened the door and entered.

It was okay to make a sort of Christmas for yourself, wasn't it? she asked herself.

She pulled a block of wood out from under the tub and stepped onto it to get in.

The water seemed much too hot, or perhaps her feet were too cold. Her feet had never known a day of warmth in this house. She stood there for several minutes, lifting one foot and then the other out of the water, cooling them with her hands, switching back and forth until she grew accustomed to the temperature. When she did, she sat down and sank deep into the tub until the water nestled against her chin.

Goosebumps formed on her legs and worked their way up to her neck until she shuddered, and in one soothing wave of heat, the warm water dissipated the goosebumps and the cold and left her feeling warm and sleepy. She lay there resting, her eyes closed, her spirit warm, and her thoughts roaming.

After a while, she gently rubbed her arms, shoulders, chest, and legs. Peter never appreciated her when she was in these moods. He was physically careful with her at the best of times and painfully careful when she was like this. He was afraid to encourage her, yet afraid to neglect her. His fearful, duty-bound hands did nothing except make her long for someone else. Peter was a sensitive man at times, but he was scared that in dealing with her he might open a door that would never close. He had taken her away from her small town, and she admired and thanked him for that. But boredom and invisibility had entered her soul. After living here with him for even a short while, she had resigned herself to experiencing her womanhood without him.

So, alone, late in the afternoon on Christmas Eve, before her husband and children returned, she celebrated Christmas in the bath. She could tolerate things after that, she thought.

The children would of course stay out for hours if they had their way. As they grew older, the breaks from chores around the farm were few and far between, and they appreciated those precious breaks more each year. They would return hungry and excited, and she would have hot chocolate and meat pie ready for them. She had even managed to get Irish Cream for Peter.

She leaned her head back to relax and tried to remember why she had been in such a rush. What had possessed her? If only she had simply said, "Let's wait to get married. What's the hurry?" she probably wouldn't be an older woman with three children living in the middle of nowhere.

Boys had seemed interested back then, but mostly with her large breasts. She had let a few older boys go too far with her, and suddenly all the boys in the county were interested in her. She stopped dating. Then at Christmas, a boy she liked from school asked her out to a Christmas party. He borrowed his father's truck, picked her up, and took her to a deserted road. He stopped the truck and tried to kiss her. She got mad and resisted at first but didn't stay mad. Then she somehow found herself rushing to put her coat and skirt back on and straighten herself up as the county sheriff flashed his lights behind them. He gave them a warning and then told them to move along. They arrived at the party late, and as the evening wore on, it seemed like everyone found out about what had happened.

Even her father heard shortly thereafter.

"You are grounded, young lady!" her father had yelled. He raised his hand several times but talked himself out of hitting her. She had never seen him so angry. "What the hell is wrong with you?" he screamed at her. "You had better not ask to go out for a very long time. And how about finding some common sense in that head of yours?"

At the co-op in town where she worked it seemed like every boy and man who came in winked at her. And one day, her boss put his hands on her behind in the back room.

It was a year and a half later before her life settled at all, and then she met one of the nicest men she had ever known. He was a few years older and such a gentleman. A year later they married. She really could not explain the hurry.

When she married and moved in with Peter on his farm, some of the boys in the county heard rumours that Peter had gotten himself a wild one from the city. One Saturday night at a neighbor's corn roast, a couple of the drunk boys who had been so nice to her escorted her to the barn. She had to call Peter for help. That night some other boys showed up at the end of their driveway after they left the corn roast. She could not quite make out what they were saying, but it was clear they were hoping she would join them outside. Peter chased them away, but it left him scathed. He handled her with growing fear and concern. And as she tried harder to love him, he became more reserved and more restrained. Her showing physical enjoyment petrified him, so she stopped physical reactions and affections.

When she first moved here she poured herself into her new life. She raised the few pigs and chickens they had and gardened the two acres surrounding three sides of the house. Money was tight. She pickled and jarred many fruits and vegetables for the winter months and made sauces and pies, which she froze. She took on the accounting and bookkeeping. She read the *Farmer's Quarterly* and sent in letters asking for advice on how to reduce debts and loans. She visited other farmers who were growing beets and soya. She learned about selling futures and tracked them for the best time to sell. She regularly asked Peter's best friend for advice when their crops were poor. She read about soil testing methods and convinced Peter they had to switch manures and fertilizers to increase the boron in their soil. Their crops improved. Peter's best friend, who farmed in a nearby county, became a regular visitor in their home and stayed for dinner many Saturday nights. She found herself looking forward to seeing him more than anything. He occasionally slept over when he had too much to drink. She found that it was all she could do to stay in her own bed. Then one night she went to him.

"No," he whispered gently.

Or did she imagine that? She wasn't sure. Things over the years had all become one fuzzy thought that rolled into the next . . . and everything was getting mixed up.

It was okay to live with a man and stay married even if you didn't fully love him as much as possible, wasn't it? Perhaps love was nothing more than having children with a man you respected . . . a good man. Surely children were the result of love. How could her heart be so cold and indifferent? So what if these thoughts were in her head? It wasn't good to fuss too much about things anyway. Besides, she had married expecting her love to grow. She had tried to get excited about Peter and about their first Christmas together. Despite knowing they had to be concerned about every dollar, she had bought herself some lingerie. It was her gift to him. It made Peter worry. She never wore it. He was suspicious that Christmastime put her into these odd moods he didn't understand. He approached her carefully.

"Now, Nancy, we ain't going to go crazy on Christmases anymore or nothing the like, you understand?"

"Sure, Pete, I understand."

Surely it was okay to not love Christmas. It was a depressing time of year for her. Everything was always so much work and effort. For what? In no time it was all over. What was the point?

She let herself stay slouched in the warm water.

The warmth eased her mind, but her body grew tense as she braced her legs in longing . . .

Then the tension slowly dissipated in the warmth, and her thoughts turned back to Christmas Eve and putting up their Christmas tree.

The children would return. Peter would get the tree to stand up straight in a tree holder that was crooked, and he would put the tree near the front entrance where the ceiling was highest. The children would excitedly pick out spots where she would place small white candles. She, as the mother, would carefully attach the candles to the end of the branches so that when they were lit nothing would burn. The children would make the star for the tree with small pinecones they had collected, cedar twigs, and candles. Peter would put it up as the final gesture of finishing the tree. Together, as a family, they all would light the candles. She, as the loving wife and mother she wasn't, would lead the singing of "Fah Who Foraze, Welcome Christmas," her children's favourite Christmas song since they saw *The Grinch Who Stole Christmas*.

Surely it was okay before putting the children to bed to lift them up so that they could make a Christmas wish come true by blowing out a candle at the top of the tree. It was okay to want them to wish for something other than what they had. Okay to kiss them gently with as much passion as she could muster, even if she didn't feel like it. As a mother, she would cup their warm faces in her cold hands and wish them a Merry Christmas and try to mean it. As a wife, she would take hold of Peter's hand, and together they would put out the candles on the table centrepiece. After all, they should each have their wishes too. Surely it was okay to kiss him as well and wish him a Merry Christmas, not just because he was her husband, but because he was a good man. What did it matter if she was up half the night, lying perfectly still, trying not to breathe, hoping that her efforts not to breathe would exhaust her and bring on sleep.

Why should it matter if she lay there dreaming, hoping,

and trying not to move? It was natural to feel displaced, as if this wasn't her home, these weren't her children, these weren't her hands or legs, nor was this her voice singing or her lips kissing . . . and this wasn't her life.

And as she grew older, her mind was playing tricks on her, for as her youngest grew, he looked more and more like Peter's best friend. Or did she imagine that too?

She no longer knew. Everything had been spinning, shifting, changing, and deserting her. Everything seemed blurred, as if her mind orbited around some confused thought.

Was that not what Christmas was about? she wondered. An expression of confusion? A mockery of her wishes for it to be otherwise?

Over the years, everything within her melted together into one feeling. A feeling of dizziness . . . as if her memories were from someone else's life . . . her thoughts from someone else's mind, her sensations from someone else's body . . .

Surely it was okay to sit back and dream of something different, a different Christmas Eve, a Christmas Eve where peace was not just among men, but in her own heart and mind. Surely it was okay to sit back and dream . . . surely that was okay . . . wasn't it?

"Merry Christmas," a voice from inside said, as if her Christmas was already over.

She knew she would soon get out of the bath to get things ready.

"Merry Christmas," she answered, afraid that for her it was true.

She lay back in the water and closed her eyes.

Soon she thought she could hear the truck turn into the driveway and approach the back of the house. She could hear Peter's deep voice and her children's laughter and excitement. She thought she heard them talk about the tobogganing, the snow, their presents, and decorating the Christmas tree.

Then, when they stepped inside, she heard them sing . . .

Fah who for-aze, Dah who dor-aze,
Welcome Christmas, Come this way,
Fah who for-aze, Dah who dor-aze,
Welcome Christmas, Christmas Day.

Welcome, welcome, Fah who-rah-mus
Welcome, welcome, Dah who-dah-mus
Christmas Day is in our grasp
So long as we have hands to clasp.

Fah who for-aze, Dah who dor-aze,
Welcome Christmas, Bring your cheer,
Fah who for-aze, Dah who dor-aze,
Welcome all who's far and near.

Fah who for-aze, Dah who dor-aze,
Welcome Christmas, Come this way,
Fah who for-aze, Dah who dor-aze,
Welcome Christmas, Christmas Day.

Christmas in So-Cal

Eighty-three days to St. Patrick's Day.

That's what the sign says. Check it each time I come here. I like knowing. First thing I look at when I sit down. It's high enough over the bar that most people probably miss it. But I'm sitting at a table by the open doors between the patio and the bar, so it's easy to see from here. The Santa Anas are blowing, so it has been windy but really warm. I mean, it's the twenty-fourth of December. Some locals are wearing summer dresses, shorts, and sandals. I guess it's warm enough and all, but still, it's winter. This time of year the heat doesn't last. In these parts, though, you get used to people in shorts walking beside others wearing fur coats and mitts . . . at least this time of year in Beverly Hills.

I mean, don't get me wrong, I'm enjoying the heat like everyone else, but I still have shoes on and long pants. In fact, I sort of have one foot out on the patio with the sun baking down on it. The sun feels good. I guess I could have worn my sandals, but I didn't. It's kind of a fashion crime this time of year on Rodeo Drive and on this little cobblestone street called Via Rodeo. That's where this bar and patio is. I used to sit at the bar but got tired of chatting it up with and listening to the bartender. Besides, with the TV going, I'd sit there forever watching football, baseball, basketball, hockey . . . ah, any sport really. I stopped that. Sit here now, at the door. Have a couple and get out.

I like this bar. It's Irish-style, and they even have Irish people working here: Declan behind the bar, and Terri over there

147

serving drinks. Unfortunately, the first time I ordered from her, I asked for Guinness. I haven't ordered since. I sit down; she brings me a Guinness.

"Another, luv?" she asks me.

That's Terri.

I smile.

It's a little better than usual today. Frankly, I don't have the heart to tell her the Guinness isn't that good here. That's the problem with stout. It's great or it's lousy. She is quite good looking and flirts with me when I'm alone, I think because I'm Irish myself . . . So I drink Guinness. It makes her feel good to know what I want. I normally drink Bass Ale when the Guinness isn't good, but the Bass Ale isn't that good here either. Of course, I don't have the heart to tell her any of that. What the hell, gotta drink something. So, she'll get me another Guinness, I'll drink it slowly, it's all just as well. Lord knows, when the Guinness is good, I drink a lot more than I should. It's not like I get plastered and become obnoxious, no, not me; I get plastered and become as still as a sleeping babe in his mother's arms. Brood a little, loud the odd time, but usually quiet and sad. Not sad enough to cry or anything like that, just sad like when you're alone. Especially around Christmas and St. Patrick's Day. Don't know why really. Hate that green-beer crap though, have to tell you.

I usually come here every couple of weeks, but frankly, as I said, the Guinness has never really been good enough to get carried away. And I'm early today. That's my second I just ordered, and it's half an hour before I'm supposed to meet Christine. My wife and I are going over to Chris and Christine's tonight for dinner. Having a beer after buying my wife her Christmas gift has gotten to be a ritual for me. Started doing it years ago.

"Thanks."

Terri just put another Guinness in front of me. Excuse me for a moment, just want to take a sip.

"Ahhh . . ."

You know, it really is a bit better than usual. Perhaps the

Bass Ale won't be so watery. Maybe I'll order it for Christine when she comes and have a sip of it myself.

So, as I was saying, shopping and coming here is a tradition for me. Actually, in truth it started when I was with my first wife. She ran off with my best friend a few years ago. Tried to tell me her relationship with him had nothing to do with her leaving me. I wasn't good enough for her, she said. Guess I was some kind of loser.

"If Michael wasn't around, I would still go my own way," she said. "I've changed, I've grown . . ."

Right. Like I didn't. Left me behind, she tells me.

"It's a growth issue, an issue of what kind of life I want to live," she said.

Right. And who does she move in with when she leaves? Take a wild guess.

"You've got problems you won't even admit to yourself," she said to me, as if I was miserable or something.

For a while I believed her, sort of. I mean, she could be convincing, she was pretty smart. Never cut me any slack, though. Said I was insecure and needed to work at myself. And if that isn't enough to hear from your wife, she said I was dishonest too. I mean, things could always be better, I grant you that, but we were doing all right. Minor problems—fine tuning. Then Michael says he's in love with her. Suddenly, I'm dishonest and a loser.

Right. She leaves me . . . wasn't good enough anymore and not the man she thought I was. Had her eyes opened, she said. Not all of a sudden, but gradually over a few years. Says I'm a closed, insecure person.

Had nothing to do with me, I say. Sure we had our problems, everybody does. Then she runs off with my best friend. The rest is all bullshit.

Excuse me, I need a hefty one.

"Ahhh . . ."

That's better. Got myself worked up there.

Where was I? Oh yeah, having a beer after shopping for my

wife's gift. That's my second wife, of course. Her name is Karen. I met her and stuff when I was married. Got together a few years back, and we've been so happy since. She's a great girl really. Honest, straightforward—like me, when it comes down to it. Just shoot from the hip . . . both of us. That's the way it is.

So, I'm having a beer here after buying my wife something at Chanel on Rodeo Drive. Karen thinks Rodeo is too touristy now for shopping, but I don't. I still like shopping here. It seems so glamorous and decadent. Makes you feel pampered, spoilt really. Like you've made it. Something like being able to drink all the orange juice you want in the morning—that kind of feeling. And after, I can sit here and have a couple of beers to celebrate. Of course, I'm never sure if she'll like what I bought her or just politely say it's "nice"—an insidious term she uses when she thinks she should like something but doesn't. Hate it when something is "nice." I want her to be speechless . . . that's best with her. I've never pulled it off, not yet. But I'm a romantic at heart. I think that's why I get all worked up and find this shopping business difficult and sad. This year I bought her gift in record time, though.

You have to understand that shopping to buy something for her is difficult for me. Always been that way, even with my first wife. So that's why I like to have a beer afterward. It helps me like what I bought. Probably need that more now since I bought her gift at the first store I went into, off the first rack I really looked at. I sit until this uncomfortable feeling goes away. It's not quite a feeling of buyer's regret; it's more a feeling of a husband not sure he bought something his wife will like. I always get this feeling whenever I'm buying something special for Karen. Don't know why really.

I mean, it isn't the three thousand it cost that makes me hesitate. Frankly, for me, buying something for my wife for Christmas is the hardest thing in the world. It's not that she's difficult to buy for either. She always seems to like what I get her. It's just this feeling that the gifts don't mean what they used to. Had the same feeling with my first wife.

So this year I wanted something special. Something she would love. Not just like, mind you, but I mean something to knock her over, so she suddenly feels great about us . . . that type of gift. Leave her speechless. I mean, she likes what I buy her, maybe even a lot, but nothing like before we were married. Or nothing like how she loves what our friends Chris and Christine buy her every Christmas. With their gift she is always speechless. It's always perfect, her favourite, as if each year they reach into Karen's heart and buy her exactly what she longs for. Each year after she opens what they get her, my gift seems pathetic, as if I just didn't put enough into it. I ask myself, Why didn't I think of that? My gift is a definite downer after that. Last year they bought her a designer dress, Armani stuff, just suited her like nothing else. Loves to wear it, and she is stunning in it. Sexy, elegant— wow stuff. The year before they bought her these wind chimes, artisan stuff, a set of seven of them for the breakfast patio, all various pitches and tones. They are like works of art each one, and the sound out of them is incredible, like a percussion symphony or something. She smiles every morning when the wind touches them.

I mean, if they can buy her things like that, so can I, I figure. It shouldn't be difficult, yet every year I come to Rodeo Drive here in Beverly Hills and feel like some kind of homeless person, as if I didn't belong. I like the street, the shops, the people. It's all beautiful, but I can't relate to any of it when it comes to picking out something for my wife. I usually go into several shops and stand in front of stunning stuff. It's as if I can never put my finger on something for her. I mean, something that she will love. I don't know what it is really. The windows here are beautiful, and the dresses are stunning, but I get sad.

Shopping for her is depressing. Was the same with my first wife. Worse than having too many beers. I mean, it's not like Karen returns the stuff I buy or anything like that, or even complains. It's just that it doesn't speak to her the way I'd like it to. I mean, you may need underwear when you're growing up as a teenager, but when your mother buys it for you for Christmas, it doesn't speak to you, like say when the girl you just started dating buys it for you. Now that's a statement. You don't know what the hell it says, but it says a lot. As if she whispered to you: "Yeah, I know I've been fighting you off recently and haven't been letting you do stuff, but all of that's going to change." See? That's the kind of gift I want for my wife.

So today, I just marched into Chanel, went upstairs and over to the far end of the store, and was standing there minding my own business when I picked up this lovely cape-type coat that was long and flowing, like in the movies. It was taupe-green, a color I don't see often. I mean, I have a tee shirt that color, or almost . . . wear it all the time . . .

Excuse me, just want another sip.

"Ahhh . . ."

It's pretty good today, have to tell you.

So there I was, minding my own business, when my hands took hold of this beautiful coat on a hanger, and unthinkingly I held it against myself, up by my chin. Don't know what the hell I was thinking. I mean, did I think it would fit or something? Who the hell knows. Once I realized what I was doing, I tried to quickly put it back on the rack, but it didn't work—these salespeople have eyes in the back of their heads and can see around corners.

"I don't know if we have your size," said the short but well-dressed saleswoman, "but the color is good on you."

Don't know where she came from.

I just shook my head. What was I going to say?

"It's a stunning coat," she continued. "Subtle, understated . . . but stunning in its elegance. She could wear it with blue jeans or out to the AA."

That's Academy Awards in these parts.

This woman was a professional. A pure professional.

"Yes," I agreed.

And I stood there, looking at it, staring at the Chanel buttons that adorned it.

She stood there, a real professional, pressuring me ever so gently with her warm smile and smooth legs.

"I have to think about it," I said to her.

"Indeed, take time. It's more beautiful the longer you look at it. It has a certain timelessness. Can I get you a coffee?" she asked.

See? Pure professional.

"No, no thanks," I said.

She was attractive in her own way, but mostly because she dressed so well and had good legs. I didn't tell her that, though.

"Go ahead and look after this woman," I said, pointing to another customer. "I'll just take a few moments."

And I stood there, looking at it. It was lovely. But was it like the wind chimes? Or the Armani?

The Chanel saleswoman was busy trying to listen to a short, heavyset woman's complaints that the boots she was trying on were too high up on her leg.

"They are too big, look," she said, sticking her leg out.

"That's the style," the saleswoman said. "You're right, though, your legs look a little short in those boots. Legs like yours should be revealed more. How about something similar in style, but not as high-cut and with a different heel?"

See? Pure professional.

I don't know how much longer I stood there. But she came over to me again with her softly pressuring smile. I simply couldn't make up my mind. Would my wife love it? That's what I wanted to know.

She stood there, waiting for me to speak, but I didn't know what to say.

She did.

She held out a package of sheer, dark green stockings, fancy stuff. The type you wear with a garter belt.

"Ask your wife to put it on with only the stockings, nothing else. It will be the perfect Christmas gift, I assure you."

See? Pure professional. It was that image of my wife that sold me, and of course I bought the eighty-five dollar stockings too. Perfect match.

But now, sitting here in the bar afterward, I don't know . .

I feel so out of place shopping for my wife. Always depresses me. Don't know why really. There are so many things I should want to see her wearing that you think I could get over this. But I sit here, beer on the table, my perfectly wrapped gift in its Chanel bag on the chair across from me, as if it were someone joining me, like I'm speaking to it or something. I can keep an eye on it, still look around, and if I happen to change my mind, it's over there, where I can leave it if I'm too embarrassed to take it back to that woman.

Excuse me again. I need a couple of sips.

"Hah . . ."

I think the first one was a better temperature. This one seems a little too cold, but still better than usual. A chocolatey brown head, a touch of molasses on the nose, a smattering of sour vinegar as well. It's the mouth feel, though, that is no good. Ah, what the hell, I complain too much, but for Guinness, it is a little thin.

So I guess it's a pretty good coat. My wife is a little tired of me buying her lingerie stuff all the time. But I figured she'd think I still thought she was attractive. I mean, she looks better than a lot of those models in magazines.

"It would be nice to wear in public the occasional gift you bought me," she said.

I mix it up a little more since then. I wasn't too sensitive with stuff like that. I'm better now, for the most part. I think the problem with those gifts over the years—and I'm being honest, you understand—the problem was that I always found it easier to buy something for my side-dish than for my wife. I mean, even with my first wife; I could nail down a perfect gift every time for a side-dish. I couldn't wait to see them in these outfits. I just kind of knew what to get; it was the most obvious and easiest gift to buy. Then, to tell you the truth, when I was struggling with what to get Karen a couple of Christmases ago (like I would come up blank for days and weeks), I just bought her some lingerie. I mean, this difficulty always confused the hell out of me. Why was it so damn easy to buy for someone I was seeing as a side-dish and so difficult to buy something for my wife? Never understood that really. I mean, I don't do that other stuff on the side now, not lately. So this year I thought buying a gift would be easier, but no. I mean, sure, I picked up her gift, but I'm not sure it's right.

Declan here at the bar has a theory, though, about why husbands find it difficult to buy for their wife but not for their side-dish. I mean, you think it would be the other way around, but not to Declan. And don't think I was advertising this stuff around or anything; we were just talking man to man, about men in general, over a beer. I mentioned this problem in passing, without naming particulars, you understand. Course you know every Irish bartender is a half-poet, a half-philosopher, or a goddamned rebel. Declan's no rebel, he just shoots straight from the hip, he says. His theory is this:

"It's always easier for a man to buy his mistress the perfect gift 'cause he sees only the good side of loving her. She will love whatever he buys her. And he doesn't have to put up with the rest that comes with being married. His mind is clear and into it. Whereas when buying for his wife, he knows that she thinks his ideas about fashion are from another planet, or at least disconnected from the time we have on earth, and he knows that no matter what he buys, it will be questioned, criticized, not really appreciated, and usually returned. What man wouldn't be daunted by that?" he asked me.

Have to tell you, though, not a poetic bone in his Irish body. Mind you, a head full of ideas and theories about why everyone does what they do. That's why I don't sit so much at the bar anymore. Between the TV and him, I got a little tired of hearing what I was supposed to think. Makes the head weary, frankly. Can't think worth a dime after that. But that was one of his good ones. But I don't do that side-dish stuff anymore really. I mean, I don't know why I did it in the first place all those years . . . just a go-for-it kind of thing. Guess a bit of my father coming out.

Hang on, I need a few more sips before my lips fall off from clacking my uppers.

"Ahhh . . ."

I mean, you think you are in love. There are voices telling you so many things, maybe right, maybe wrong, but you got to fall in love with someone and have a wife. Who the hell knows what they feel for sure? And who the hell wants to be alone? So it feels like a duck, sounds like a duck, so we call it love. No big deal. But what about all this other side-dish stuff then? What's that about you ask? Well, you know it's not love, but to hell with it. Feels good, a boost to the spirits so to speak, and don't think about it after that. That's where beer helps, if you ask me. Maybe even the TV and sports. Puts the mind at ease.

Just a minute again.

Sorry, I needed a big one there.

But the stuff on the side is over now. I stopped that. For good. Course Terri flirts with me and would go for it, but I stopped that. It's not that I've been running around or even been dishonest, it's just that I started feeling funny . . . like Karen and me weren't as close. Don't know why really.

Ah, there's Christine. Just a minute . . .

"Hello there."

I kiss her cheek. She never really kisses me, just makes a kissing noise beside my head, you know, near my ear.

"How about a beer? A Sam Adams or a Bass Ale?"

"What are you having?" she asks.

"Guinness."

"Maybe I'll have a Sam . . . whatever," she says.

"Sam Adams," I say to Terri, who is walking by me. Terri's awfully careful when someone is with me.

"So, were you successful?" Christine asks.

"Yes," I say and try to sound proud. "I got something in record time too."

"Should I wait till tonight to see it? Or should I sneak a peek now?"

"It's kind of wrapped."

"So it is," she says, looking beside her at the bag. "Chanel, very nice."

Terri put a beer on the table in front of Christine.

"To Christmas traditions," Christine says.

We raise our glasses.

I like cheering or toasting, whatever you call it. Kind of sets a mood when you are about to partake. Don't usually do it myself, but it's really nice—

Wow.

She just took an incredibly large gulp. Something's up.

I wait. She takes a couple more sips. Big ones.

"Are we in a hurry?" I ask jokingly.

"Mmmm . . . I have some things to do for dinner when we get to my place. I didn't get as much time to prepare dinner as I wanted. But Chris will probably be shortly behind us and can have a drink with you while you're waiting. You'll be glad to know you got your way; we'll be barbecuing the lamb tonight."

"Ahhh . . ." I always clap my hands together. It bugs Christine. I seem to do it more and louder around her than anyone.

I take a couple of large gulps myself; she is drinking hers in record time.

"Did you want to get going now?" I ask. "We don't have to finish."

"Well, the sooner the better. Would you mind?"

"Not at all. Maybe I can help, and we'll have time for a drink together—just you and me."

Don't know why I said it in that kind of suggestive tone. I mean, she is great looking, and I have thought about it lots, especially when we've had a few drinks or we've been in the pool and she's in a bathing suit, but I've never really spoken to her that way. A couple of times I even tried to peek down her top or kiss her lips—bump against her, hug her, that sort of stuff.

She stares right at me.

"Well, I could use some help," she says, looking at me suspiciously.

I thought at one time she kind of liked me, but maybe I was wrong. I mean, at one time I thought she wanted me to look down her top and touch her and stuff—

She gets up.

I do too. Throw some money on the table.

"Merry Christmas," I hear Terri and Declan say.

I nod and wave.

Christine looks at me oddly as we get to the car. Her house is about fifteen minutes away, and she drives in silence.

When she turns onto her street, she suddenly stops the car.

"You know, I've been attracted to others here and there over the years, but I've been faithful to Chris, even lately, though things have been off. I'm convinced at this point that he is having an affair. I still love him deeply. I plan on being faithful to him until I feel otherwise. I just won't do that to someone I love, not even if he is doing it to me."

"Yeah," I say. "You're right. Me either."

I mean, what am I supposed to do? The woman is claiming some kind of virtue. What the hell. And besides, it could have been true, 'cause I'm thinking more and more like that, and I've stopped stuff. Don't know why I bothered with all the side-dishes anyways. Just don't know really.

"So," she says, "unless you know something I don't and think I'm somehow available, I'm not sure what you were suggesting back there. Perhaps Chris has mentioned something."

"No, no, not at all. He hasn't and wouldn't talk to me about any of that. It was nothing. I mean, I was just flirting, sort of, nothing meant. I'm sorry. It's Christmas, and I was feeling so good about what I bought Karen. I mean, she will look great in it. Never really been that fortunate. Usually I get buyer's regret with whatever I buy her. She's so damn hard to buy for."

She starts driving the car slowly down the street and pulls into the driveway.

"I mean, I think she'll really like it. Shopping was fun this year," I say as we get out of the car.

She just nods her head.

"I'm starting to feel like you guys, you know, enjoying it and stuff. I was just kind of going with that, that's all, Christine."

"I see," she says.

When people are upset or mad at me, Jesus, I get really uncomfortable and just about crawl out of my skin. And of course I'm Irish and tend to just go on at the mouth.

Ah, guess you noticed.

We approach the house.

"I like our traditions together," I say. She is still a little sore at me. "I mean, it's great that we have dinner on Christmas Eve with you guys, open gifts and all that . . . It's always so much fun . . . you guys are such great friends."

She nods and fumbles for her keys as we get to the door.

I mean, I'm trying anything so that we won't be in an off mood to start. Nothing worse really. I hate it when someone is feeling bad about something I said, especially a woman, and especially when you got to spend time together.

"So, how did your shopping go today?" I ask her.

"Not bad," she says.

"You always seem to know what to buy. Chris always loves what you get him. How do you do that? I mean, Karen's favourite gift every year without fail is what you guys buy for her. It's always perfect. It's a talent. How do you know what to buy her? It's like you read her mind."

"Well, actually, Chris buys for Karen. Has for the past couple of years now. He'd be pleased to know that she likes what he buys for her. He really tries to get Karen something very special."

Son of a bitch, I think.

I don't say anything.

She puts her key into the lock and opens the door.

"Oh," she says, looking at the shoes by the door, "looks like Chris is home already. Maybe you can have a drink with him while I get some things done."

I nod.

"Merry Christmas," I hear Karen say from up the stairs.

She is sipping a martini and coming down the stairs with glowing cheeks and a big smile.

"Just doing some last-minute wrapping," she says.

She kisses Christine and turns to me.

"Merry Christmas. I'm glad we all made it a little early. We'll have more time to celebrate," she says.

"Celebrate, what?" I ask.

She laughs.

"Christmas, what else?"

I hate being uncomfortable and I'm as uncomfortable as hell.

"I thought we were celebrating the fact that it is now only eighty-three days till St. Patrick's Day."

What the hell else am I to say?

I kiss Karen's warm lips and find myself looking at Christine's ass as I follow her into the kitchen to help.

Midnight Christmas

What is Mrs. Jenkins doing in my office? I asked myself.

How am I to explain to anyone the mixed feelings I have about a patient who makes me wonder why I ever became a doctor? And of course, she had to show up the day before Christmas.

Christmas Eve has always been a bone of contention between my husband and me. In the past, seeing patients the day before Christmas has always meant one rush after another, with everyone coming in to make sure they are well enough to enjoy the holidays. Of all my busy days, it's one of my busiest. When it is over, I simply have no energy left.

Not this year, though. I closed the office early. Had coffeecake and donuts for my staff at lunch time. Small gifts too. It's the first year I couldn't afford bonuses for them. Felt like a heel because they work so hard for me, but it's pathetic these days. Instead, I sent them home at lunch and added a couple of days off to the holiday. Yet somehow Mrs. Jenkins got in here. She makes me wonder why I bother.

When I was really young I thought I wanted to be a veterinarian, mostly because I loved kittens. But at the age of ten, when an aunt was visiting—relatives just showed up at the door as I remember it—I was permitted to watch her breast-feeding her newborn. I remember sitting beside her on the bed. She pulled her baby away from her breast for a moment and asked me to hold her.

"Your mom told me you wanted to be a veterinarian. You

may want to keep in mind that there aren't enough doctors around," she said.

I held the baby and then watched it suckle . . . guess I was sold. Later in high school, I worked hard at math and science so that I could apply to medical school.

My parents were doing okay, but they were not that well off, so I worked at a grocery store some weeknights and weekends to help pay my way. I mean, I got loans like everyone else, but I tried to keep that to a minimum. Worked like a dog to make it through, though. Yet even now, I sometimes wonder why I still do this. After practicing for fifteen years, you'd expect you wouldn't think such things, but you do. And then Mrs. Jenkins showing up in my office can make me feel as if I should just drop it all and do something else. Honestly, I never liked her. I got a bad feeling about her twelve or so years ago during the first appointment.

Yet I'm supposed to be her doctor anyway.

There are numerous things about her that I just don't like. She stinks. Isn't clean, doesn't care to be. Never once followed any of my advice. Is argumentative. A good percentage of whatever she has recently eaten is always spattered on her clothes. She wears her deceased husband's threadbare polyester pants, which are too tight for her paunch, which bulges through the broken fly. She acts twenty years older than she is, as if she wants to be old and dying. Not only does she waste my time because she's lonely, but she outright lies. I don't know what to do with her. I have many times counseled her to find another doctor. I even reached the point of telling her that I didn't like her or want to treat her.

"I ask you to seriously consider finding another doctor," I once said to her.

"Are you going to call the police if I come here when I need a doctor?"

Let me tell you, the urge to lie was almost overwhelming. But I'm a lousy liar, and then I'd be like her.

"No," I said, "I'm not going to call the police. You should find another doctor, though."

Didn't see her for a while, so I thought it had worked. But she came back. And now she's sitting there in my waiting room.

I took the first resentful step toward her.

"My office is closed," I said.

She didn't respond.

"I'm just on my way home, Mrs. Jenkins."

Again, nothing.

I walked to the front door and opened it. I thought I would see if she was prepared to be locked in. Apparently she was; she didn't move. So I stood in the hallway in front of my office, looking out over the open courtyard below. She has unbelievable gall, I thought. I don't seem to have an extra ten minutes in my day, yet she wastes more of my time than anyone. I hate putting up with that, especially around Christmastime.

If you think I'm a little sensitive about my time at Christmas, you're right. I actually want to spend a Christmas Eve with my husband and children. Maybe it's all the memories of my dad or something, but I think it's important. My dad would stagger home late Christmas Eve, drunk, of course. Mom would have us ready for photos in front of the tree for hours . . . you think she would have learned. It seemed like every year we waited and stood around the tree most of the night. Sometimes we had hot chocolate with marshmallows. Long after we were in bed, Dad would clamour into the house, staggering and slobbering his way toward the washroom, then to bed. It was terrible. My dad fancied himself a drinker, but there was one problem with his fancy: he couldn't hold liquor. Didn't matter how much or what, he was sick to his stomach every time.

When I started a family, I swore I wouldn't miss the things my dad seemed to, yet I haven't made it home at a proper hour on Christmas Eve since I opened my own practice. As a child, I don't think I minded the drinking so much as him not being there. These past years, I've been so tired at Christmas that I may as well not be there. What's the difference? I mean, I get up with everyone, but I'm exhausted beyond zombiehood, even while drinking cup after cup of coffee. Most Christmas mornings I end up back in bed. They open gifts and I'm gone . . . I get into the Christmas spirit sometimes on Boxing Day . . .

Not this year.

"Only one gift for the children this year," my husband said to me. "And we're celebrating Christmas on Christmas Eve; it's a German tradition. No ifs, ands, or buts."

My husband thinks of himself as German, but his parents are Canadian, so were his grandparents. Maybe his great-great-grandparents were actually from Germany, but he's Canadian through and through.

"And don't buy me any gift. Your gift to me will be the evening together."

I looked back at Mrs. Jenkins. I know what my daughter would say about someone who drove her crazy: "She makes me mental."

I looked out over the courtyard to calm myself.

It is a stunning setting. It was the reason I opened the office here. My office is in a medical building shaped like a square box, except the centre has been cored. The entrance to the building leads to a courtyard. Open staircases in the corners and open corridors along the inside of the courtyard take you to each of the four floors that surround it. There is an elevator in one corner and a pharmacy. The offices are not very exciting, but the courtyard is. At one end of the courtyard, opposite my office, there is this larger-than-life, Asian-styled sculpture. It is a nude woman with hair smoothly flowing around her head. She is squatting on a rock, with shoulders leaning in, knees apart, and arms running down the inside of each leg. Her hands are open, palms up, slightly overlapping each other on the rock. Her eyes are closed. She is calm, peaceful, tranquil. Sculpted into the space above her hands and below her breast is a child, standing with its arms to each side. The child is looking out at the world with wonder. It could be a boy or girl; I've never been able to tell. I start most of my mornings with a coffee in hand, standing here, looking at her. It is then that I understand wanting to be a doctor.

Okay, I'll see what Mrs. Jenkins wants. Her usual complaint

is lower-back pain. What's aggravating is that she won't have it X-rayed and won't show up if you book an appointment to have it looked at. Won't exercise, walk, warm soak it, or do anything else I suggest. Basically, she wants to be assured that she is okay without doing a damn thing. To put it mildly, this wasn't exactly why I spent nine years at school.

I took a deep breath and walked toward her.

"So, what can I do for you, Mrs. Jenkins?"

"My arm," she said without looking at me.

"What's wrong with it?"

"Hurts," she said.

"Well, step into the examination room, and I'll have a look."

"Rather you looked here."

I took another deep breath. I didn't say anything, and despite a strong urge to yank her arm, I was genuinely careful and gentle.

"I don't see anything. Where exactly does it hurt?" I asked.

She lightly tapped her wrist with her finger.

I took hold of her arm carefully.

She felt warm. Too warm, I thought. It was cold out there today.

"Do you feel warm?" I asked.

She didn't say anything. Hated to speak.

I felt her forehead. She seemed hot.

I couldn't tell if the wrist was swollen, but it didn't look right.

"Let's go into the other room; I'll be able to see if we have a problem."

I didn't wait for her to answer. I left her there, opened the examination room, and turned on the light. I waited a few moments, then decided to give up. I went back to the waiting room, and she was standing, holding onto the arm of the chair with her good hand. She wasn't moving.

"Is your back sore?" I asked her.

She nodded.

I took her good arm and helped her into the examination

room. There was no point in asking her to take off her clothes so that I could take a look at her; she wouldn't. She was obviously not able to move well, and I helped her lean against the examination table. There I could see that her wrist was indeed red and quite swollen. I tried to feel it; she was in obvious discomfort. I felt her forehead again, took her temperature, pulse, and blood pressure. Her temperature was a little high, but her pulse and blood pressure were not bad.

"How long ago did you hurt it?"

"Few days," she said.

"How did you hurt it?" I asked.

"Slipped," she said. She was holding herself at the hip.

"Goodness . . . on some ice?"

"On stairs," she said.

"A few days ago? Good heavens. Were you able to get up on your own and walk around okay?"

She didn't answer.

"How long were you on the stairs, Mrs. Jenkins?"

Again she didn't answer.

"Have you been dizzy or having hot flashes, Mrs. Jenkins?"

No response.

"Undo your blouse and pants, Mrs. Jenkins," I said, raising my voice to command her into action, "I want to take a look at you."

I waited a couple of moments for her to start to take off her blouse and trousers. She didn't move.

"Have you been experiencing vaginal dryness, Mrs. Jenkins?"

She just looked at me with a scowl on her face.

"Have you been regular with your period?"

She wouldn't answer.

"Look, I need to know. Do you still have periods, Mrs. Jenkins?"

She looked sad, and I thought she might cry.

My God, I thought to myself, she doesn't understand.

"How long ago did your periods stop, Mrs. Jenkins?"

She looked down at the floor.

Could be years, I thought.

"Stay right here, Mrs. Jenkins, I'll be right back."

I stepped into my secretary's office and shut the door. For once I was glad there was a door to that office.

I called 911 to get an ambulance. Then I called the local hospital emergency ward.

"I have called an ambulance, and we should be there soon. Got a patient coming in who needs X-rays on the left arm and hip area . . . maybe lower back too. Hip's probably broken . . . elderly woman . . . likely Osteoporosis . . . gotta have someone look at her right away. Broken maybe a few days . . . who knows if she's bleeding in there . . . can't examine her properly. She can't hardly move, and I don't know how the hell she got to my office. Yes, that's me, just up the street from you. Should be there shortly."

I walked back into the examination room.

"Mrs. Jenkins, I have to get some help on this. You may have broken your hip and your wrist. Bones sometimes get brittle when we get older, especially after menopause, so I have to take you to a hospital. Do you understand?"

She did not answer.

You have to know, I couldn't leave her. I stayed with her till I don't know what time. She wouldn't let anyone touch her otherwise. The local anaesthetic didn't work so they had to put her under to reset her wrist. She was weak, and I helped out in the emergency ward while I was waiting for her to come around. After all, they attended to her as soon as I got her in there. Badly broken wrist, three hairline fractures around the hip . . . the poor dear. I stayed around to make sure she was okay. She had never been to a hospital before. I mean, I left her in good hands, but she was pretty shook up. I stayed and talked to her, told her what to expect and how she was going to be in there for a little while . . . hell of a way to spend Christmas. I'll get in to see her when I can . . . maybe tomorrow.

It was sometime after twelve when I got home. Can't say I thought about how angry my husband would be till I got in the car and noticed the time on my way home. I should have called

. . . I just honestly didn't think of it. I get on one track often, and it's all I can handle . . .

I missed the photos by the tree, the apple cider, the German Stollen that Omma taught him to make, as well as the children lighting the candles on the Christmas tree.

Oh well, what can you do?

I entered the house from the garage, and it was pretty dark and quiet. I took off my shoes, rubbed my face, and thought of pouring myself a drink but decided not to. I was beyond exhausted and wasn't sure how I had driven home. Somehow I made it up the stairs. I was almost in tears, imagining what my bed would feel like. Just to get off my feet and feel my head on my pillow—

"Ouch!!! What the hell—" I asked myself.

Something was pricking my feet. I pulled out all kinds of pine needles that had stabbed through my knee-high stockings. That hurt. I felt like cursing but reminded myself to keep a civil tongue as I opened the door to the bedroom.

And there they were. All of them. My husband and the two children sleeping on the bed. They had even brought the Weller Ten-Year-Old Bourbon Whiskey upstairs so that I could have a drink. The Christmas tree was placed near the end of the bed. The decorations were a little crooked, and there were pine needles all over the rug, but they had carried it and all the gifts up here. Christopher clutched a long match in his little hand as he slept, and Lauren hugged her pillow.

I went over to my husband and put my lips on his.

"Froehliche Weihnachten," I said as he awoke.

He tiredly smiled and took me in his arms.

"Merry Christmas," he whispered.

"Hey," he said, raising his voice to wake up Christopher and Lauren. "Hey, let's start this party. Come on, you deadheads . . . let's light the tree so we can open some gifts."

What could I do? No matter how tired I was, I just didn't want to miss it. I skipped the bourbon and had a warm apple cider instead. We sang Christmas carols, lit the candles on the tree, and watched Christopher and Lauren in their pyjamas bounce on the bed in the candlelight until they settled enough to open gifts.

Of course I bought them more than one gift . . . and I bought my husband a Krups expresso machine . . . with German coffee too.

He seemed rather pleased, even if I fell asleep shortly thereafter.

Words in Season

.

Black Figs

"We don't like'em," my wife and children say from the table
    to my offer of dessert from the kitchen.

I picked them off our tree this morning,
    out back, perfectly ripe.

They've been on the vine since November,
    contemplating me.
It's a short fig tree, barely six feet in height.

Grows
Succulent, whispery-sweet, plumlike figs,
I polish them with sunflower oil.

Bright purple with streaks of olive green,
    kissed by plenty of California sunlight.
I make a small, star-shaped incision;
    they will burst open like blooming, dark red rosebuds.

"We don't want any," voices echo in the dining room,
    when asked if votes are final.

It's a late dessert this Christmas.

I flame the stove and warm the Chambord
    to make an angel's sauce,
Place the figs in the pan
    to poach in liquored raspberry.

Pour the angel sauce onto a plate covered with fresh,
    shredded coconut, shavings of Belgian chocolate,
And homemade ice cream.

Carefully, arrange my black figs like a crown:
Opaque purple, black, red, with mysterious powers.

Sit at the table and eat,
   deaf to contrary pleas.

"We didn't know that's how you eat them," they weep.

   So fresh, luscious, and sweet.

Christmas Beer

"Get the chicken wire," my dad said.
He pointed to the corner where he had it on a spool.

His work shed was his beer kitchen.
Mom wouldn't let him brew in the house.
He makes such a mess, she says.
So we go to the shed to help him and have a sip or two.

Besides women, my dad likes three things best:
Bread, butter, and beer.

Although he eats a lot of bread and puts butter on everything,
We suspect he likes beer best;
    We never tell him that, though.
    He never asks—we leave well enough alone.

Me and my brother John collect green and brown bottles
    All through the year—
Wine, whiskey, anything fancy, and clay-baked jugs too.

Save the nice ones for Dad's Christmas beer.
He makes a gift of it for neighbors, friends, and Uncle Joe.

Christmas beer meant he put the frozen fruit,
    Unused from last year's picking, into his beer buckets.
This year he added raspberries.
    The buckets have been sitting in the shed for a month or two.

Uncle Joe gives Dad the barley, his best, he says,
In exchange for a couple of buckets of Dad's best brew.

Loving beer for Dad meant

Year to year he'd try something new.
"An annual crap-shoot," Uncle Joe calls it.

Some years, people phone for orders all around the county.
    Other years, Dad does all the calling.

Mom says John and I can't have any,
    But Dad hates to drink alone;
Pours us each a tumbler in his shed,
    Looking disappointed that we weren't girls.

We stay quiet; we're not in the shed for conversation.

Mom won't let Dad keep the beer in the house anymore.
Me and John put too much sugar in the bottles last year.
Better carbonation—extra fermentation, Dad said.

On Christmas Eve Dad put a crate of bottles under the tree;
Uncle Joe put a cage with a live hen on the crate of beer.

Glass, feathers, cork, chicken, pine needles,
    And decorations everywhere.
    What a mess. Mom was so upset.
Dad keeps the bottles away from the house now.
    This year we didn't add as much sugar.

Now we're helping Dad wrap the bottles with chicken wire.
    "Wrap them tight, boys," he said.
The ones for gifts we weave with ribbon—
    There's a lot of them . . .
The phone has been ringing this year.
    Word gets around fast.

Me and John place our tumblers on the bench
    Like Uncle Joe does, with nothing said,
Hoping Dad will fill them
    Now that his mood is good with Christmas cheer.

Ann

With no E

Lit a candle on Christmas
When she was alone.
In the afternoon, before dinner,
Upstairs; by herself in her room.

Her favourite time of year.

She put on her burgundy velvet dress,
With white vest, laced over-top;
Stood straight, closed her eyes,
And wished Christmas to last.

Dad and Mom would no longer
Head into a long night
And bitter morn casting
Shadows across the floor.

It was a sacred wish,
One saved up each year.

She was growing tall for twelve years old.
Brushed her hair in front of the mirror,
Chin raised, like her mother,
Pleased with how she looked without marks.

The boys all thought her pretty,
Though none would near.
The girls all thought her nice,
Though nice was never made clear.

And she tried to look her best
For Christmas Day and dinner.

Everyone seemed so happy.

For popular was Ann with no E—
Family, relatives, parent's friends,
And many at school.

Even if they did not understand
That from this day forward,
Her thoughts she would abide,
No more shadows, disgrace, tears, or lies.

"No more—" she stated with determination.

It was the end of her inner doubt,
A disgrace of fault she thought her own.
The end of her popularity,
The end of being nice—and insincere.

Thinking mattered most, she decided,
Instead of what pleased others.

Her parent's friends, relatives
Blinked in rhythm, mouths gaped,
A sort of disbelief, though they knew

These bruises made in anger,
A cloak-and-dagger excuse,
Fists, knuckle-white,
Face, battered tears,
Swollen, oozing—and in fear.

And her own friends too, and sister—
Disappeared with everyone else.
CRACK: truth spoken.
Bing—Bang—Boom—salute.

No turning for Ann with no E,
No backward step to take,
The world was out there living
A grace to earn, her place.

And this was the start of her lifelong idea.

To spend Christmases in candlelight,
*   With others who agreed,*
That Christmas was a promise kept—
*   Near the heart*
Throughout—year after year.

The Frost

Waits for me
Like I wait for the sun.

My father waited here,
too long,
became cold, strange.
Alone.
Eyes glazed over.

It's like that here in the far north,
with snowdrifts, snow fences, and ski-doos.

He wanted to be here
'cause he was afraid of people.
Though he'd say nature called,
and this was nature's due.

Now I'm in his place,
sitting at the window
in the same chair,
with the same thoughts.

Here, on his island in the snow,
trying to be at home
as a winter-wonderland recluse.

As if that's how things
were meant to be
for my father,
and now me.

As if nature were a replacement

181

for these things inside
we don't quite understand,
yet feel,
and try to hide.
Alone.
Here,
as the frost creeps toward us.

The Darkness of Dawn

It's night at the window,
  Inside and out
Darkness strikes this little girl's eye
Bitterness in thought and intent
  An edge and harshness, rarely kind.

Softened—
  With carols being sung
  Baked goods in the oven
  A warm fire burning
  Christmas lights on, and
  Presents under the tree.

  Christmas stockings hanging,
  Hot cider, cinnamon sticks
  Cold snow flurries falling
  Frost on her bedroom window
  Melting against her lips, and
  Kittens meowing at the door.

Growing up and growing tall,
  yet young enough to want her childhood
She whispers promises and asks for gifts
  Silent and aloud. And often sings.

  When in bed she wonders
  What Christmases will be like
  With friends and kittens
  And lots of snow rides,
  Not these family things.

When it gets late and no one makes a sound

She wishes for a future, aloud
In which the darkness in her eye is still,
And the darkness in the sky
   Does not leave her lonely when she stands
    Sleepless, at the window sill.

Friends of Eigensinn

A set table is an alter,
    For lips to kiss the night
        Dining room candles burn
            On tree mushrooms mounted on the walls
              To chase the forest shadows away.

Bread placed by windows, sliced
On logs around the room
The fire in the fireplace roaring
Creating a grill this night too.

    Passion seeps from pores,
        Around the table with close friends
            In the to and fro of life's pantry
              . . . we meet here, again.

A large chevre ravioli
In spiced carrot broth with burnt rosemary twig
Morel soup, served in a nest
With a quail's cluster of eggs.

    In sharpness of clear sight
        When decisions are made in life,
          Lay thy soul here
             . . . before this alter, stay.

Heated foie gras created by heavenly hand
Of butter, armagnac, and starry eye
Kisses its way down, inside, to meet winter
Accompanied by brown potato pancakes.

We cannot breath.

Our thoughts won't let us,
We want only this . . . nothing more.

This dining room table is an entrance
  To a restless life in tune,
      We sing better here,
          Shaped by plate and discourse
                  hands and lips held, loved, longed
                      —around this table we live.

All business and bitterness forgotten
There is a sea-serpent delight sailing toward us
Nestled in a tarragon cream
Scallop, squid, shrimp
Fresh water clam and escorting capers.

Again, we wish to breath but cannot
Except only through this dish
We will have only this . . . nothing more.

  Candles are changed.
      Breads replenished.
          Water, wine . . . refilled.
              Has it been two hours since?

A small pork loin, grilled at the fireplace
Hot crab-apple relish with pears and currants
And bits of fried boar in our mashed potatoes
Crowned with roasted garlic.

Stop. Try to breathe.
This is our favourite.
We want only this . . . and more of it.

Yes, a break.

A glass of wine. No.
    Iced sorbet; to clear the palate,
        Wild plum and tart choke cherry
            Served on frozen dandelions
                Wildflowers, daisies in ice.

A walk in the woods.
No. Too much snow this time of year.

To hell with walking,
    Let's have more potatoes, relish, and pork loin.
        Let's storm the kitchen this minute.
            No. You are right, my dear.
                A walk to the barn. Yes,
                    Breathe; sing carols there.

Hot apple cider awaits our voices.
Soothing us, preparing us for more.
Did we sing for an hour?
No, it was a moment in the sky
We were lifted to where there is no time.

We must go back.
    The main course awaits,
        Someone says and pulls our arms.
            The aroma strikes us even from out here
                In this dance-hall barn.

We race.

Venison grilled to a luscious burgundy-red
Three fanned on a plate with red-wine jus
Baby beets and onions, pearls
Spätzle with croutons,
And a dollop of foie gras.

Ah. This is it.
　　　We want only this . . . nothing more.

We decide we will marry this chef,
　　tonight, in the dance-hall
　　　　with moonlight reflecting off miles of snow,
　　　　　　glimmering through the knotholes
　　　　　　　like silver candles
　　　　　　　　　lighting this cloudless night.

　　　　　To the barn
　　Carry candles, wine, and the two we shall marry
　　　　—Michael and Nobuyo—
　　Singing, dancing, hugging each other and the air
　　　　　What's this?
　　　　He has anticipated us.

Dessert is waiting there around a bonfire,
　　An outdoor cafe table of frozen log and stone,
　　　　Sweet barquettes filled with Belgian chocolate,
　　　　　Surrounded with crème fra"che
　　　　　　Swimming in brou de noix

　　　　Four of us curse with delight.
　　　　　Five cry.
　　　　Nine of us kneel.

"I do," someone says.
　"We do," we all chime in.
　　　Hugs turn to kisses, words, and wines exchanged,
　　　　Smiles, handshakes, kisses, silence, praise.

　　　　Stop what you do.
　　　　No matter.

Listen
Breathe
Come now.
This moment awaits.

Lips kiss lips, then smack the air and sky,
In conscience clear with each life setting
Glasses lifted high in friendship,
Cheer, in heaven,
. . . here, at Eigensinn Farm
Where as friends . . . we all belong . . .
yet again, and again, and nothing more.

Grampa's Chair

Was a point of contention.
He would sit rocking for hours, whistling, singing
In the living room, beside the window,
Overlooking his favourite field beyond the stone fence.

> His chair was hard, dark, heavy and smooth.
> My brother and me on Grandpa's knee
> > Would rub the stubble on his face.

> He enjoyed his tea there, weak,
> sipping from the saucer.

Strong tea that Mom made he'd drown with milk and sugar.

He let us have some from the cup he never used,
Lukewarm, sometimes cool. We never complained.
Dad and Mom didn't want us to stunt our growth drinking tea.

We loved Grampa,
> but we never let him cut our hair,
> even though he wanted to.
> He cut Dad's clean off, left him with none,
> except on his nose, eyebrows, ears.

Christmas we opened gifts in the morning,
> at Grampa's feet.

This past summer Grampa left us for the field, Dad says.
> That's where he spread his ashes,
> > right out there.

Then my brother saw Grampa's chair rocking.

Swore it was true, even with the thrashing
        Dad gave him, twice.

Saw it, he said
till Dad took Grampa's rocking chair away.

I guess to Grampa's favourite field,
        beyond the stone fence,
To where he had so often
        tended, tilled, and then stared.

"Socks"

I said to my mom.
She asked what I want for Christmas.

> *I'm too old for the toys I really want,*
> *Too young for the girl I really need.*

Christmastime is like a Friday afternoon at school,
> *Full of hope*
That something will happen with Jacqueline,
> *A girl in grade eight.*

> *I haven't asked her to the Christmas dance,*
> *I don't know if she would,*
> > *I just wish I'd grow.*

> *She's a grade ahead and a head taller.*
> > *It doesn't look good.*
> *I bought her a scarf*
> > *but don't know when to give it.*

> > *Never see her alone.*

It's awkward getting older, still too short and young for girls
> *And I regret losing rights to toys.*

> *"Act your age. You're no longer a little boy."*

Mom won't buy me the laser gun I want,
So why not ask for a pair of socks I just don't need.

> *Besides, Mom wouldn't really want to know*
> *What I'd like for Christmas.*

As if she were ever twelve,
    Or even remembered her teens.

Christmas Boots

"We can't afford it," Mom had said.

Now, wet, at the porch door,
    Smelling of street and grime, tarred wood too,
        holding up for Mom to see.

Looking tattered and worn, scraped, maybe a little small.
    Not too bad, though, she could tell,
        but she was not pleased.

Smiling though the dirt,
    proud I had found what we could not afford.
"Found it by the old bridge," I said.

Shabby, dirty, mud all over, with nicks, scratches,
    missing patches, and oil stains on the toes.

Limp and rubbery for being neglected and left out
    in rain and snow,
        unable to stand, flopping down to one side
            at the ankles.

"Outside," Mom shouted. "Too dirty to bring in here."

    Kept in the work shed, saved what I could;
        it was my Christmas gift this year.

Every day got out the brush and would have used soap
    or shampoo had we the right kind.
Patience it took, like making a new friend,
    I nourished, brushed, and made clean.

And then on Christmas Eve,
in a large open box with tissue,
under the tree,
I put this kitten I call Boots.

Christmas Cards

Greetings, from the paper boy.
Joy and Peace to the World,
 the water company wishes.

May you and yours share a Happy Holiday,
 a postcard included with our electrical bill.

Drive safely, our car lease company requests.
Enjoy these special days, a thought from our mortgage trust.

May all your wishes come true,
 that's our credit card and bank, sending duplicates.

Season's Greetings, from our gardeners,
Meowy Christmas, from our vet.

Eat, drink, and be merry . . . from Trader Joe's.

Christmas Cheers, toasts The Wine Club,
To you and yours and those who are close,
Barnes and Noble, and Borders Books wish.

Enjoy your first Christmas in your new home,
 that's our real-estate agent, Peggy.

Don't drink and drive, stay alert and fit;
 that's our health club.

A warm and safe holiday to all, from the gas company.
Remember those less fortunate,
 the paralyzed veterans remind us.

There is friendship in the face of a flower,
    and a flower for each friend;
            that's our neighborhood florist.

Take care this holiday season, from State Farm,
To your good health in the New Year,
    our HMO doctors salute.

Buy a child in need a gift; offer them hope,
National Public Radio cards plea.
We know that Good Will is more than a dream.

The music clubs each wish us well with offers,
As do all and every mail-order service we've ever used,
And many we haven't do much the same,
    till we are swamped with brochures, magazines,
    and Christmas cards, both old and new.

And every card, every wish,
like angels offering blessings
To the season, our neighborhood, house and home.

We put them around the entrance door,
With Dad and Mom's card
    like a halo at the top,
Sisters', brothers', cards cherished
    along strings to and fro,
  All wishing us love, warmth, and happiness.

Yet we sit here, so many miles away,
anxious at our friends' contrast
Waiting for these others that have not arrived
Even though Christmas has long past.

December Far Away

Silence breathes out back
Under the California sun.
We feel the warmth, sip our coffee,
On our rose garden patio.

We are new to this
Sunny Christmas, coats in a box,

December so far, far away.

Here, roses are in bloom,
Oranges and lemons in the trees,
The Italian figs ripen black,
Camellias bloom from morning mist,
and warm afternoon sun's kiss.

Beyond our window there are wires and lines
and rows of telephone poles,
Beyond that many snow-peaked mountains,
yet no ringing of the phone.

The air is still, except for birds,
Using phone lines with skill.

Sitting out back in our garden patio
In sunny warmth and silences,
remembering Decembers far away.

In heated, cold rooms shared,
Hidden, with both faces,
Pressed back to back to back
Coventry and palter played,

With each other,
    as if this were a game.

There are no roses, oranges, lemons, figs,
No flowering blooms to see or smell,
    No fire.

    And nothing on their lips or laps
    To help smooth over this sadness,
    Helpless victims, hopeless feelings,
    Never stop to see the facts.

For it was a December long ago, so far away
    That drove them to their hate
When they confused fear with love,
    And invited others . . .
                    . . . to share in their fate.

Christmas Tea

Our grandmother used to add cloves, almonds,
   orange and lemon peel, cinnamon and allspice
      to the boiling water
         on Christmas Day.

   A bag for every person, and
      two for the pot.

   We were a large family,
      strong tea she made.

Lots of milk and sugar passed our way
      till it was creamy beige.
         Except at Christmas,
            some of us would drink it plain.

   Nice cups, even for us, as if we were
   guests. Biscuits, jellies, dried fruit
   and clotted cream on raisin pie,
   that our Aunt Jeanne made.

   It was a High Tea celebration
   For us in the dining room.
   In our house we were not often guests,
   except Christmas Day, at noon.

My Wheels

After my two brothers' gifts were unwrapped,
The paper cleared,
Mom made us eat breakfast.

My gift had only a bow;
It was something to behold.
Red, white, blue.
Nothing too fancy, but it was a mountain bike—
sleek, shiny, new.

Gulped down my juice,
Swallowed pieces of orange and banana whole,
Rolled up my toast and shoved it in.
It hurt going down—all the way.
Felt funny once it landed.
I didn't care.
Grabbed my new wheels and was out the door.

Christmas Day was always warm,
sunny, quiet on our street.
I rode . . . as fast as I could.
The breeze blowing against my face,
Bugs—and bees too—bouncing off my chest,
One in my shirt, stung my bellybutton,
Swelled like a balloon.
Swallowed some gnats on the way home
Cleared my throat the rest of the morning
'cause they stuck there, even after more juice.

In the afternoon I picked her up with my new bike
and rode up Grapevine Road into the foothills.
My belly hurt when I pushed on each pedal
to get to the top of the dirt road.

From there, we looked back on the streets below,
our house, my dad walking along the driveway,
my brothers wrestling out back.

Only on Christmas Day does Mom let me come here.
It's where the rowdies hang out, down the road,
They beat up an old man once, stole his car,
Burned an old shed, not far from here,
a fence and small field too.

But I've been here many times on my own,
Mom and Dad don't know.
Smoked my first cigarette here,
First fistfight too.
Kissed her, French-style, the first week of school.
She took off her shirt under our favourite tree,
but I wasn't exactly sure what to do.

Then she was caught stealing pencils in class.
Had them in her desk, neatly placed in rows, like in a store.
She was bad, our fifth-grade teacher said,
Mom and Dad too.

So I didn't tell anyone I liked her,
Even though I picked her up on my new bike.
Her, behind me, sharing the small seat,
hugging me as we rode my new wheels
along Grapevine Road to our favourite tree.
From there we threw rocks at the birds, downhill,
Smoked cigarettes she stole from her brother's stash,
And kissed, French-style,
Though I'm not exactly sure what to do.

The Snowdrifts of Aladdin Island

There are nine of us here. Friends.
A small inlet, part of northern Lake Nipissing,
Where the wind creates drifts across the bay, even in November.
Parked cars. Tobogganed supplies.
Ourselves in snowshoes to the island
          For New Year's Eve.

Only the kitchen of the cottage is insulated.
We huddle there, where most will sleep.

The woodstove hot, fireplace burning logs,
The outside drops to serious below.
This was expected. The weather here has no sympathy,
No human compassion for New Year's Eve.
It was less cold when we dug our way in.
Buried in snow, the cottage will stay warm,
But will we?

We've all agreed,
If it gets colder than fifty below, we leave.
The next morning is nasty, but the midday warms
To minus twenty-one.

We build a huge igloo at the end of the dock,
Over the ice,
Pile snow there, as high and wide as we can,
Put boards on it to stomp it down,
All of us, piling snow, until the mound is wide, hard, high.

We place long twigs into it, at equal depth,
Dig it out until we reach those twigs.

We dig quickly at first, all of us,
But with no intention of doing too much,
Making sure our enthused boy scout
      ends up with the only good shovel.

He does the digging, as we planned,
      let's leave him for a while.

Drink scotch instead. Scotch is not good for boy scouts.
Besides, we have dinner on our minds too, and beer.
And I have getting out of my ski suit since putting on
      ten pounds over the years.

Put many candles in the igloo when our boy scout's work is done,
Offer him a beer. After all, boy scouts need nourishment and
      a little bit of cheer.
Our igloo will be warm for our midnight toast to
      each other and the New Year.

At night, waiting to pop the champagne,
We look into each other's eyes with love, warmth,
      and some disdain.

It's odd being a close friend to thee.
I know unclear things, ill intent, sarcasm, even fear.

Mature men with girl-watching habits, hoping a look,
      wink, or nod will get them something unnamed.

And late-night drinks and affairs,
Sanctioned by a lack of shame.
Distractions with unknown but sought little girls,
      and magazines bare,

Wishing for a different mate when,
Just putting in time there.

Knowing too—
Disappointments with these men lacking passion.

And a soap-opera affair with yet another boss,
denied in tears year after year after year.

Uncertainty swirls the wind around our igloo
of friendship, lies of snowflakes pile up,
grow heavy, and are pressing on these walls,
Creating snowdrifts, especially for those so wantonly unaware.

I want to say something, as if I'm the wall with ears
Against which these drifts start, develop, and grow heavy.

But who am I? Another deceived with other snowdrifts,
denied, of course, in honesty.
I should scream.
I don't. I'm silent like the rest, despite thinking I have
something to say, something to blast these
snowdrifting, isolated walls away.

I don't know why I cannot speak.
I announce I will and stomp my foot,
but still my voice will not thunder,
nor will my boot.

These drifts seem like the ice: thick, deep,
Too premeditated.
A sort of self-blindness shared, offered,
and accepted by all,
Though nothing is made clear.

And there are nine of us in all. In our igloo
sipping scotch, waiting for the pop of champagne,
Huddled together by candlelight,

Sharing cigars, breath, kisses, hugs,
  and just the right amount of disdain.
Holding up our glasses
  For the right moment to cheer.
  For we are silent mostly. After all,
It's snowdrift smiles we've exchanged
  over many years.

Nine of us . . . friends . . . until the spring, when
This feeling of friendship,
Like the winter, igloo, ice, and snow,
Will melt, melt, melt away.

Too Young and Old

I have to admit, I get tired.
Maybe I had children too late;
*   didn't start till forty.*

"Dad, we have to put up our Christmas lights."

I just don't have the energy I used to.
The lights and decorations,
Sometimes I think we should just leave
*   everything up all year round.*

"Come on, Dad."

Like she helps, being eleven.
Although she has a voice like a whip.

"Right now, Dad. Come on. Don't be a deadhead again.
Christmas is coming."

A lifetime of getting more tired year by year.
I have to say, I get more excited about an afternoon
*   nap than I do about most things.*

"Come on, Dad. I'll help you with the ladder."

I say what I always say, "Okay, okay,"
Knowing that the lights outside are but the start of my little girl's
*   idea of Christmas decorations throughout the house.*
*   It never ends. She's an idea child, bent on shaping my fate.*
I grab my coat and mitts . . .

"And we have to have a hot chocolate and decorate the tree.

When we finish, Mom's going to read us a story. Hurry up."

Perhaps I could have a nap on top of the ladder,
Or when looking for the tree decorations in the attic;
It's cold there, but the insulation is thick and soft at least,
*   although quite prickly, even through these winter clothes.*

*   Please don't ask.*

It's strange to think how warm and cozy the word "nap"
*   makes me feel.*

Yet I too as a child got up, stayed up, and treated each moment
*   of every day as if I would miss a once-in-a-lifetime*
*   adventure, a secret entrance opening for only a moment.*

Now I wish I could find that entrance myself.
I suspect there would be a couch,
Or perhaps a cloudlike bed, hidden,
*   away from this ladder, these lights, and the little*
*   dictator at the bottom of the stairs.*

"Come on, Dad. We're the only ones without lights up on
*   the whooole street."*

As if I care.

But for her, I do.
She is my angel, after all.
Her smile is attached to mine,
My heart it gently taps
She is warm, kind, full of life and love—
I only wish she'd learn to take naps.

Christmas Cake

That my mother bakes
Whispers to me from the freezer.
In the kitchen, downstairs.

She sends me two every year:
One dark, I soak in brandy
One light, I soak in amaretto.

Each evening,
After everyone is asleep,
"Come," they say, "eat, drink, and be merry."

I make my way down the stairs to the kitchen.
I can't refuse these voices of childhood, youth, and holidays,
Guiding me with heavenly hand
To creations that await
Making each day complete.

Cut a thick piece from both,
Savour even the smallest crumb of
Fruit, nuts, cake, spirits, as one.
Smack my lips with satisfaction,
Pat my proverbial back,
Rub my non-proverbial belly.

The world is a rather fine place;
Life is sweet.

Quietly creep up the stairs
To where my wife has barely moved.

Slip back into bed,
As if I hadn't been gone,

Make a pretence of rolling over after a moment
To reclaim the blankets from me robbed.

She lifts her head and looks at me,
One eye open, finger pointing,
"In the morning, you jog."

Boxing Day

It's late afternoon, time to act.
The girls are asleep on the couch,
Nestled under some blankets.

Like sisters, the three of them,
Heads on shoulders in hugs, eyes closed.
Newspapers strewn across their laps.

We make a little noise,
Walk by with waving hands,
They are asleep.

We have waited for this moment.
I give the nod; we ignite as one
Into action, comrades-in-arms.

Our boots, coats,
Quickly, our glasses,
Quietly, the bottle of scotch
From the coffee table.

A sip or two in the afternoon together
Outside, even though it's cold.
A few more jokes and stories to share,
The holiday does not end untold.

Wait. Stop. Don't move. Not a sound.

An eye opened on the couch,
As if it sensed the scotch we took.
"In the kitchen," we were commanded.
It was our turn to cook.

Bibliography

Campbell, Reginald J. *The Story of Christmas*. New York: Macmillan Press, 1934.

Golby, J. M., and Purdue, A. W. *The Making of the Modern Christmas*. Georgia: University of Georgia Press, 1986.

Hottes, Alfred Carl. *1001 Christmas Facts and Fancies*. New York: De La Mare Co. Inc., 1944.

Martin, Judith. *Miss Manners' Guide to Excruciatingly Correct Behavior*. Page 521. New York: Galahad Books, 1991.

Miller, Daniel (ed.). *Unwrapping Christmas*. New York: Claredon Press, 1993.

Nissenbaum, Stephen. *The Battle for Christmas*. New York: Alfred A. Knopt, 1996.

Restad, L. Pene. *Christmas in America: A History*. Oxford: Oxford University Press, 1995.

Tennant, Eugenia L. *American Christmases from the Puritans to the Victorians*. New York: Exposition-Banner, 1975.

$\mathcal{D}.\ \mathcal{J}.\ \mathcal{St}.\ \mathcal{A}mant$ has spent many years as a technical writer for computer software firms, as well as writing novels, short stories, and poetry. Originally from Canada, he now lives in California and enjoys good food, good wine, and time with his family.